Christi,
It's awesome time!
Go for it!!
Jim Smith
9/18/09

From
AVERAGE
to
AWESOME

From AVERAGE to AWESOME

2nd Edition

41 *plus* gifts in 41 *plus* years

JIM SMITH, JR.

Foreword by LES BROWN

Beaver's Pond Press, Inc.
Edina, Minnesota

ISBN 13: 978-1-59298-099-4
ISBN 10: 1-59298-099-6

Library of Congress Catalog Number: 2005900547

Jacket Photography by Pat Harmon (Photos with Personality)

Printed in the United States of America

First Printing: February 2005
Second Printing: April 2005

09 08 07 06 05   6 5 4 3 2

Beaver's Pond Press, Inc.
7104 Ohms Lane, Suite 216
Edina, MN 55439
(952) 829-8818
www.BeaversPondPress.com

To order, visit *www.BookHouseFulfillment.com* or call 1-800-901-3480. Reseller discounts available.

JIMPACT Enterprises
1530 Locust Street, #161
Philadelphia, PA 19102
www.jimpact.com
jimsmithjr@jimpact.com

This book is dedicated to my mother, R. Nanci Smith. Mom, you gave me life, my spirit, my drive and my passion for helping others to become awesome. I owe everything to you. Thank you for your love, your lessons and for your never-ending support. I can ALWAYS count on you! I'm so proud to be your son! You are indeed one of a kind.

CONTENTS

Foreword, xi
Acknowledgments, xiii
Introduction, 1

Gift ONE:
File, Save, Open, and Print, 9

Gift TWO:
Savor Your Moments, 19

Gift THREE:
Remember Your Titans, 29

Gift FOUR:
Get Mad, Get Sad, Get Better, Get Busy, 37

Gift FIVE:
Ready, Aim, Fire Up an Awesome Day, 45

Gift SIX:
Fire Hard, Kid, 53

Gift SEVEN:
Start Playing More Reader Rabbit, 59
Awesome Reflections Page, 64

Gift EIGHT:
Stop Depositing Bad Checks, 65

Gift NINE:
Say Cheese!, 75

Gift TEN:
Wear Your Own Jersey, 81

Gift ELEVEN:
Say What You Mean and Mean What You Say, 87

Gift TWELVE:
Let Your Light Shine, 91

Gift THIRTEEN:
Believe You Can Fly, 97

Gift FOURTEEN:
Some People are Just Not Going to Clap, 105

Gift FIFTEEN:
Be Yourself, Because Everyone Else is Taken, 113

Gift SIXTEEN:
You're Not Always Going to Get the Best Hand, 119

Gift SEVENTEEN:
Ssssshhhh…Listen to Your Own Advice, 129

Gift EIGHTEEN:
Have a Forgiving Spirit, 135
Awesome Reflections Page, 144

Gift NINTEEN:
Remember That the Cure for the Pain is in the Pain, 145

Gift TWENTY:
Start With the Wing First!, 153

Gift TWENTY-ONE:
Know That It's Not Always All About You, 159

Gift TWENTY-TWO:
Dance Like Nobody's Watching, 169

Gift TWENTY-THREE:
Listen to the Music, 177

Gift **TWENTY-FOUR**:
Be Hungreee, 183

Gift **TWENTY-FIVE**:
Keep Your Glasses Clean, 191

Gift **TWENTY-SIX**:
Wow Yourself, 199

Gift **TWENTY-SEVEN**:
Get the Junk Out of YOUR Trunk, 205

Gift **TWENTY-EIGHT**:
Enjoy Your Awesome Journey, 213
Awesome Reflections Page, 219

Gift **TWENTY-NINE**:
Understand That Awesome Challenges ALWAYS Await You, 221

The 41 Plus *Gifts, 229*
Personal Awesome Action Page, 233
Take the 30-Day Awesome Challenge, 241
About the Author, 245

You'll find more gifts as you read the book. These gifts come in the shape of powerful thoughts or quotes within each chapter. Each of these gifts has a gift box in front of it. Additional gifts are the opening chapter thoughts and the end of chapter Extra Awesome Gift testimonials.

JUST TO GET YOU THINKING...

Not that success, for him, is sure, infallible.
But never has he been afraid to reach.
His lesions are legion.
But reaching is his rule.

—Gwendolyn Brooks

I have never been contained
except I made the prison.

—Mari Evans

If you have no confidence in self you
are twice defeated in the race of life.
With confidence, you have won even
before you have started.

—Marcus Garvey

FOREWORD

It has been said that experience is the best teacher. I think that's partially true. I believe that we can avoid a lot of pain, failure and disappointments in life by learning from the positive and negative experiences of others to maximize our own growth and development in life.

This book has been written to empower you to transform your life from average to awesome. As you read and absorb each page, you will discover mind-expanding thoughts and ideas that will inspire you to soar to new heights. Exposure to the key turning points in everyday people's lives will give you knowledge and insights that will enable you to avoid some of the dangerous, treacherous waters of life and get in touch with your own purpose and mission. Jim will be the first to say that this life-skills book was written in a style and language that everybody could relate to and identify with. The messages and concepts are common sense but not common practice. I believe that most people today are seeking and searching for meaning and significance, more so than ever before. Each chapter of this book will provide you with the necessary keys to unlock the door of your unlimited potential to live a life of contribution, passion and purpose.

You owe it to yourself to take some quiet time from the noise and distractions of the world and get into this book. I guarantee you, based upon my own experience after reading it, you will never be the same again. It will change your life!

Jim you've done yourself proud!

—Les Brown
World Renowned Motivational Speaker, Best Selling Author,
Radio and Television Personality and Mrs. Mamie Brown's baby boy.

ACKNOWLEDGMENTS

I'm blessed to have so many incredible people in my life and in my corner. I refer to them as my Anchors and my Titans. Because of their unfailing strength, support, guidance, patience, love, motivation, leadership and goal and role modeling, I'm able to thrive, come alive and yes, survive. They were the keys to my completing this arduous and inspiring project. They provided counsel and "just in time" hugs and encouragement. They also gave me feedback and space to grow, to write, to fly and to continue my journey from average to awesome. Thank you so much!

MY ANCHORS

Daecia Smith (my daughter), R. Nanci Smith (my mother) and Rodney A. Smith (my brother).

MY TITANS

I have numerous Titans in my life. If I listed them all I would probably have to entitle this book, *Jim's Titans* rather than *From Average to Awesome*. Let me take this opportunity to especially acknowledge several of them: My Grandmom (Carrie Bryant), "Nana" (Mary Lee Faulks), Aunt Venessa, Aunt Cookie, Aunt Lillian, Aunt Gail, Uncle Reggie, Cousin Carol, my sister-in-law Michelle and my other wonderful family members. In addition: Gina M. Williams, Anthony Spann, Kim Forde, Kathy Cook, Raimond Honig, Yolanda Rocio-Fleming, Kimberly Cortijo, James and Veronica Gallman, Michael Thompson, Joe Boswell, Nancy Rebecca, Lynn Roman, Catherine Woods, Marilyn Massaro, Aileen Dizon, Leslie Shields, Michael Robinson, Lucretia Coleman, Brian and Raenonna Prince, Yvonne Reid-Sissons, Barbara

Stern, Patti DeRosa, Mary Ellen Russell, Mary Mueller, Lisa Nichols, Bill and Lynn Hart, Arvon and Denise Jordan, Sharon Jackson, Tracy Librick, Paul and Danielle Kallmeyer, Sherry Nottingham, John Pace, Kathy Dempsey, Deloris A. Davis, Judy Chapman, Sally Solis-Cohen, Dawn Ridenhour, Annette Stewart, Pauline Shadding, Tony Simmons, Terry Simmons, Roberta Ross, Becky Bottaro, Barry A. Callender, Bruce Scagel and the other members of the Simmons team, Anthony Graham, Kathy Gilbert, Jennifer Moore, Griff and Meena Barger, Barb Kompelein, Sandi Dufault, Leann Bohn, Keith Baudin, Diane Chew, June Becker, Bobbi Foster, Steven Myers, Jane Elliott, Steve and Judy Kane, Sonny and Meryl Elia, Sharon Gerlach, Jeanne Bray, Janae Bower, Loraine Ballard Morrill, Anita Lewis, Maria Garaitonandia, Trina Crockett, Ceasar and Evelyn Smith, Patricia Smith, Lester and Clementine Robinson. After you read the book, if you would like, you can write your name here _____. I always have room for more Titans in my life.

I also want to give a HUGE thank you to my friends, colleagues, clients and supporters who contributed to the "Extra AWESOME Gifts and Quotes" that you'll be reading in the book. Along with my Titans they are: Dr. Frank "Tick" Johnson, Adrianne M. Winter, Priscilla Shumway, Bonnie Strand, Assunta "Susie" F. Marino, Roberta Salisbury, Bettina Carey, Kimberly Reynolds, Doug "Waffleman" McCallum, Hannah G. Gomberg, Jey Willis, Joe Sparacino, Kim Schreck, Laura Bruner, Elmer Smith, Lisa Dommer, Laura Hughes, Lisa Marzullo, Barbara Rivera, Lorainne Hicks, Rajean Bifano, Paul F. Hafner, Renne Gallart, Ron Mitchell, Shannon Percy, Sheryl B. Craun, Ann Perington, Dan Kropp, Tina M. Greene, Tracie Johnson and Les Brown.

A special thank you goes out to my awesome team of editors: Doug Benson (lead editor), Ellen Godfrey, Willette Redfern, Bronwen Brown, Leslie Shields, Joe Sparacino, Kimberly Cortijo, Catherine Woods, Barb Stern, Rodney Smith, Bill Clark, Leann Bohn, Patti DeRosa and Bill Hart. We did it!

One final shout out goes to Milt Adams (Beaver's Pond Press, Inc.). Milt, you effortlessly took the publishing baton and helped me take things to an even greater level with this revised edition. You and your team are truly a gift. Thank you for being in my life. And I want to thank YOU, that's right YOU, for bringing me, through this book, into your life. ENJOY!

INTRODUCTION

Dear James,
It has been a pleasure to teach you and to know you.
Keep your ideas, your sense of responsibility, your willingness to work and
your pleasing personality—and life should be good to you.
May you have a life of service and happiness!
—Mrs. Audrey Brodie (June 23, 1979)

This book project began nearly five years ago.

I sat on the floor in a familiar position, my back leaning against the numerous authors on the bookshelf, my legs crossed, ankles overlapped. My subconscious pressed the rewind button in my brain and took me on another fascinating trip down memory lane. With my University City High School Class of '79 yearbook nestled comfortably in my lap, I turned each page in slow motion, savoring and inhaling every memory, every photo, and every signature.

Some 55 minutes later, I reached the faculty pages and there she was, beaming—my mentor, every lazy senior's nightmare, the lady who was the gatekeeper for umpteen students' diplomas or summer school plans, Mrs. Audrey Brodie.

The chairperson for the school's National Honor Society and my 12th grade English teacher, Mrs. Brodie was a treasure. With graying hair, pristine grammar, an Estelle ("Golden Girls") Getty wardrobe and as absolute as a judge demanding quiet in a noisy courtroom, she was a living institution. If educators ever created a Mount Rushmore for teachers, her face would undoubtedly be featured.

Mrs. Brodie conjugated verbs, assigned oral book reports and jackhammered English theory into students' heads as if this would be their last chance…and sadly, in many cases, it was. During her 40 plus years in the classroom she even taught former basketball legend Wilt Chamberlain.

This super teacher was the reason I majored in English in college. She was the reason my focus in graduate school was journalism. She was the reason I fell in love with Shakespeare, with poetry, with creative writing. She was the reason I knew that one day, some day, eventually, when I finally got around to it, when I stopped putting off the inevitable, I would write the book you're now reading.

While sitting there studying her words, I imagined Mrs. Brodie, propped behind her desk, directly in front of the blackboard saying, "James Smith," ("Yes Mrs. Brodie," I replied), "it's time to write your book."

After that special, reflective moment, I was on a semi-mission to write this book. I say "semi" because for the first twelve months or so, my mission consisted solely of my telling people that I was writing a book. That became *problem number one*. I told my relatives. I told my friends. I told the participants in my management development and creative training workshops. I told the people who came to hear my keynote motivational speeches. I told the people who sat next to me on the plane. I told my radio listeners who tuned in to listen to my inspirational words of wisdom each week. I told more people about my writing a book than Bob Barker's announcer has told to "Come on down," on The Price is Right.

Everyone knew Jim Smith, Jr. was writing a book…everyone but my fingers. They waited and waited and waited, patiently, painstakingly, embarrassingly for me to begin.

When I finally decided on the angle, I got recharged. I was going to write a book that was semi-autobiographical, focusing on strategies people could incorporate into their lives to be awesome at home, at work, at school, etc. I did not care that my book would be the 2,222,222,222nd self-help book. My book, I knew, was going to be different. It was going to be a combination of Les Brown and Ellis

Cose, mixed with Pat Croce, Oprah Winfrey, Richard Carlson and Dr. Wayne W. Dyer and seasoned with Iyanla Vansant and Ralph Wiley.

From a motivational and from a personal standpoint my book was going to really STRETCH the reader. The book was not going to be just your typical "rah rah," hug everyone, eat the right foods, list your top five goals and post them on the refrigerator, promise to have a better attitude for 21 consecutive days, get on the treadmill every day and say "I can do it" motivational book. My approach was going to be more visual, more personable, more poignant, more revealing and as conversational and candid as other books of this genre. Just as important, I was going to "keep it real."

Since I have enjoyed many pats on the back and have endured many kicks in the seat of my personal, academic and corporate pants, I thought my perspective might be curiously insightful, helpful and perhaps, surprising to all of my readers. I decided to share many of the hurdles I've had to clear to move from average to awesome. One of those hurdles happens to be race. During my journey to awesome, I have grown accustomed to playing the Jackie Robinson role in many of my endeavors. On academic, athletic and corporate teams, at parties, facilitating workshops or on business trips, I've learned how to fit in and how to flourish. Elaborating on this hurdle, I thought, would undoubtedly take people on a continuous 15-inch journey—the longest 15 inches in the world—the distance between one's head and one's heart.

I knew some of my readers would wonder why I decided to even mention race. They would wonder why, since I've been relatively successful in life, I have to play the race card. I knew that some of them would not understand that race was just, albeit significant, one of the MANY hurdles I had to clear and that by mentioning it I wasn't playing *the* card. I anticipated that some would simply see me as just another angry black man. Nevertheless, I decided that if I omitted the race-hurdle experiences I would be omitting a measurable part of who I am. It would be comparable to asking Ray Charles to write his autobiography or to consult on the making of the movie of his life without mentioning the role blindness has played in his life. My objective was to simply share a moving, penetrating message with readers of all walks of life. To that end, I wanted my book to be on your mind long after you put it down.

During my 43 years of breathing, I've learned a great deal about what it takes to be AWESOME from a number of sources. I've learned from my mother, and from my diverse group of Titans, mentors, colleagues and friends; you feel them throughout the book.

I've also learned through my numerous experiences while attending schools and universities that were usually predominantly black or predominantly white. I've been the president of a nearly all black student affinity group in college and I've been a captain on the football team at that same, nearly all-white, school. Ironically, I've spent my professional life mostly with white people and my personal life (early on) mostly with black people. In essence, I've consistently lived, thrived and at times barely survived, in two unique worlds.

I've been up close and personal with stabbings, muggings, poverty, drugs, roaches, water bugs and mice as well as with judges, doctors, business owners, corporate executives, lawyers, and professional athletes. It's been some ride! And through this book I'm going to share my awesome trip.

Problem number two arose. I thought the book would need a magnetic title—one that GRABBED your attention like a wallet full of money lying helplessly on a quiet street corner. The title had to be one that people would energetically repeat when they were telling others about their personal life journey. I wanted a title that had a powerful, clever, creative, yet familiar, ring. One that would make readers and bookstore customers across the world hurry to pick it up as if they were first time parents rushing to the crib to pick up their crying newborn. Unfortunately, I let this dilemma postpone my writing even longer.

Then it happened… my epiphany.

During the month of August (2001), I decided to attend a week-long workshop for entrepreneurs, held in Burbank, California. From a professional-development standpoint, this was a no-brainer: I needed to be there. From a staying-on-top-of-my-debt standpoint, I couldn't afford to take a week off. The thought of taking a break from my plane rides, workshops, speaking engagements and client commitments began to seem as ridiculous and risky as eating a tray of ice cubes in three minutes. I had to grow my business. "The workshop will have to wait for another time," I kept saying, trying to cajole myself. But something kept pulling my heart, pulling my thoughts and pulling my energy to Burbank. I sent in my enrollment check.

I promised myself that I would be the consummate student. I would sit in the front row during every session. My plan: network, observe, learn, soak up the positive energy and discover ways to grow my motivational speaking, train-the-trainer and management development business. My other "agenda item" was to develop a plan, or at least the facsimile of a blueprint, to complete my book by year's end.

The conference workshops began on Sunday. Because of other work commitments, I arrived on Monday morning as eager as a toddler at Toys R Us. And on Tuesday morning, during my first session, my enrollment check and "agenda items" were all cashed in.

Lisa Nichols, the charismatic and engaging facilitator, was leading a session on how to express your WOW (the term students were encouraged to use when referring to their goal, their dream, and their reason for being at the workshop) as clearly, as passionately and as succinctly as possible. After her captivating, empowering 45-minute overview, she scanned the audience of 285 for volunteers to come up to the front and practice our 30-second WOW. Never one to turn down an opportunity to run my mouth, I stared at her like she was a Happy Meal, sending my energy and vibes her way. Girlfriend, whether she knew it or not, **WAS** going to make eye contact with me and ask me to come up front. I didn't care how many other zealous people raised their hands. I *was* going to get Ms. Nichols' attention. I *did*.

Looking professional, poised and polished, adhering to the grooming and fashion tips I learned from my corporate, minority, professional development workshops and conferences, I wore a navy blue double-breasted suit, white pocket square, navy blue shoes and white crew-neck shirt. Ms. Nichols finally put me into the game, motioning for me to come up front. Eager and a little anxious, I tried to appear nonchalant as I emerged from my second row seat, took a deep breath and carried my truckload of self-esteem to the front of the room. I felt like I was on a roller coaster that was about to plunge.

Upon reaching the front of the room, I immediately thought to myself, "OK, Jim, here we go again, another high risk." The anticipation, however, was very exhilarating. Ms. Nichols asked me to share my WOW. Having seen the first four volunteers stumble through the routine, I felt reasonably confident. I thought for a moment, "since they each got a C on the exam, at least I know I won't fail." I was prepared to take this WOW thing to another level. I was going to be "*the man.*" The starter's pistol fired in my head! I was ready to get busy. "Here's my big chance," I thought.

To no avail, I stumbled to a hard-earned C+ in my first attempt. I spoke softly. I stumbled over a few words. I lacked my usual fire. I felt the pressure. I was way too serious. I kept saying, "I try to help people find their dreams," without mentioning how I did it or why I did it. I played not to lose rather than playing to win. Ms. Nichols dusted me off, gave me a few additional pointers, and then encouraged me to try again.

My second attempt moved the needle on the grade meter a little closer to a B, but I still had not aced this test. The appropriate words just didn't flow off my tongue as they did hers. I just didn't feel it. After the two attempts, I thought I was through. I was prepared to return to my seat, humbled yet still positive.

Then the spirited facilitator with the infectious, disarming smile, took my hand and asked me to just talk to her and the audience about my WOW. "Don't worry about the 30-second rule," she assured me, "just tell us about you and your company, what you do." After listening to my brief overview, she did her best 30-second version of what my WOW could sound like. She sounded poetic, rhythmic. She could have won a Grammy for best lyrics in a WOW. She concluded with, "Ultimately Jim, what you do is move people from average to awesome!" The audience roared with approval, my heart raced with excitement, and my mind shouted, "That's the title for your book Jim!" Needless to say, on my third attempt I put my arms around an A and squeezed tight, finishing my WOW, saying confidently and passionately for the first time, "I move people from average to awesome!"

The crowd clapped with approval and I triumphantly returned to my seat, writing the introduction for the book in my head.

So that's what I do and that's what this book is about—many of the awesome, insightful, inspirational gifts that I've acquired in 41 *plus* awesome years of life. Regardless of what you do professionally or personally, this book casually and quickly walks and talks you through lessons, keys, anecdotes, experiences, ideas and practical steps you can take to get the most out of any situation.

Why "awesome?" It's powerful! Its meaning extends so much beyond material wealth, awards and success. It's more than being the straight-A student or the first to do this or the first to do that. Its meaning goes beyond elaborate titles, too. In a nutshell, being awesome is consistently feeling fulfilled, ecstatic, positive and energized about yourself and what you do! It's a way of life.

I hope this book moves you to make the life changes you've considered before but put off until now. I hope that it moves you to think more deeply and more consistently about things you've never given much thought to until now. I hope the book asks the appropriate questions and provides the right answers.

If you encounter any skids during your reading, remember what you were taught when learning how to drive: turn into, not away from, the skid. Upon reaching the skid, read, then reread the points that stretch your beliefs and understandings. As Stephen Covey says,

"Seek to understand before you seek to be understood." To the best of your ability, attempt to walk in my shoes and the shoes of others who share their experiences in the book. At the very least, ask others for their opinions. You can even e-mail me and we can discuss any problems you might be having relating these lessons to your own life.

To help you assess and develop your action steps after reading each chapter, I've included average and awesome examples for moving forward. My Titans, colleagues and friends, people just like you from all over the United States, Mexico and Canada, share their Extra Awesome Gifts (i.e. thoughts, anecdotes and pointers for what makes them awesome) at the end of each chapter. They also share Awesome Quotes at the beginning of each chapter. In addition, I've also included a Personal Awesome Action Plan Page for you to record the five most significant awesome actions you plan to take as a result of reading that chapter. After reading a chapter, turn to your Personal Awesome Action Plan Page and record your five awesome actions. Then turn to the next chapter and continue reading! Every 60 pages or so you will come across an Awesome Reflections Page. Use this page to record exactly what you're feeling or thinking at that point in the book. No editing, just immediate reactions…flow with your thoughts.

Writing, then revising, this book was an exceptional experience, at times painful, at times therapeutic, at times exhilarating. I found the entire journey to be extremely rewarding, maturing and timely. And, I could not have done it without you, Mrs. Brodie! Thank you!

—*Jim Smith, Jr.*

GIFT

File, Save, Open, and Print

Through joy and pain, patience and persistence, I have mastered the ability to keep myself in a place that gives me inner peace with everyday life changes and trials. Maturity, time and drive are my best friends.

—Lorraine Hicks (Philadelphia, PA)

During my corporate training classes, I enjoy telling participants that I attended kindergarten through 12th grade without missing a day of school. Their reactions are nearly always the same: "Oh wow," "No way," "That's impossible," "Awesome," "Your mom must be proud of you" and "You're kidding."

I'm extremely proud of this accomplishment! It means as much to me as a gold medal means to an Olympic athlete. My perfect attendance record paved the way for my committed, disciplined and hardworking approach to life, for my belief that you can work through almost anything if you put your mind to it. After I broke my ankle in the 10th grade during a high school football game, I thought my attendance streak was over. I think I cried more about the streak being over than from the excruciating pain in my ankle. However, the next day, with books in hand and a cast on my leg, I hailed a taxi and went to school. The streak continued!

I also share this little "window-into-my-world" fact because it provides a smooth segue into talking about my mom, R. Nanci Smith, a black, single parent, who raised her two sons in Philadelphia during the '60s, '70s and '80s. She mothered us, fathered us, nurtured us, coached us and at times drove us nuts because of her structured and disciplined approach to living. She guided us to adulthood, teaching us so much about life that I'm just beginning to understand some of her lessons today.

Upon being asked to talk about her two sons, she will ease into the conversation by proudly mentioning that both of us have master's degrees. Education was always important to her.

Her influence on my life's blueprint has been profound; she's been the architect of my values, my rock-firm foundation. She stood on the sidelines, in all kinds of weather, during my Little League, high school and college games. Her attendance was as predictable as that of the cheerleaders, the referees and the umpires.

She taught me the importance of always being on time and the significance of making a powerful first and lasting impression. She would always say there's more to life than just sports. She inspired the "get involved" spirit in me. To that end, I've lived a life of making it happen rather than watching it happen. She also taught me to always: help others, sit in the front row in any class, smile for identification photos, dress my best, be respectful, get up early, make up my bed, keep thorough files, save money, live below my means, take care of myself, and make an impact in whatever I did.

She attended every parent/teacher report card meeting-night. She taught me how to balance a checkbook, how to jitterbug and how to play pinochle (she still is my favorite card partner.) But most significantly, she taught me how to reach and how to recover.

I also tell people about my perfect attendance because it was during those early years that I first learned many lessons about what it takes to be awesome. I learned how to get the most out of whatever I was doing and how to hold on tight even when life was treating me like a dart board in a crowded tavern. I always sprinted the last lap at the end of practice. I ran my "suicide drills" all-out. I walked the four mile round trip to school when our city's public transportation went on strike during the winter months of my freshman year in high school.

My younger brother, Rodney, always tells friends who are struggling through one of life's wrestling matches, "Go talk to my brother." You see, Rodney has learned plenty from my bouts with sorrow, injuries, rejection, pain, racial discrimination, corporate politics, failed relationships and broken promises. He sincerely believes that I am the poster child for life's ups and downs. "You need to go talk to my brother about that. The same thing happened to him; he'll tell you what to do," he assures the friends.

I don't know about all of that, but I'm committed to helping people move from OK to outstanding and from average to awesome. I believe we all have talents and gifts. One of my gifts just happens to be that after life smacks me around, I process, savor, shine, and then share. I file, save, retrieve, open, and then print. Recalling my experiences days, months and years later, after I have thoroughly processed and learned from them, is what really refuels my spirit. My 41 *plus* years have been tumultuous, filled with good guys and bad guys, despair, love, a bunch of "isms," prejudices, competition, stereotypes, graduation, rejection, action and celebration. I can vividly remember when:

- I was four years old and my brother was born; I spoke to my mother on the telephone while she was still in the hospital and I told her to send him back;

- my mother, brother and I squeezed into telephone booths waiting to catch the bus and trolley cars (on our way to church) during the rainy and frigid winter months;

- our living room ceiling leaked into the buckets that were placed on the floor every time it rained;

- my father used to say, before commencing the whipping with his black leather strap, that spanking me was going to hurt him more than it was going to hurt me;

- my mother would find the bottles of beer and vodka my father had hidden behind the living room sofa and television set and pour them down the toilet;

- I feared for my life during my commute to and from middle school because of the white neighborhood gang that despised people of color;

- I spent my summers with my Grandmom and Nana in South Philly;

- at age 12, I won my first trophy: the Jayhawks beat Millcreek for the Little League baseball championship;

- as a teenager, I attended the Moore College of Art on a summer internship;

- my parents divorced;

- I was All-Public in three sports (honorable mention All-City in two);

- I attended nearly all-white Widener University;

- I dropped an interception in the closing minutes of the Division III National Championship college football game between Widener and the University of Dayton;

- I graduated from Widener with a Bachelor of Arts degree in English. I was the first in my family to earn a degree (and then couldn't find a job!);

- my mother earned her college degree;

- my high school sweetheart and fiancée ended our five-year relationship one month after I graduated from college;

- I was cut from the professional football teams I tried out for;

- I was married by a Justice of the Peace, just four months after meeting my wife and less than a year after graduating from college. I also became a stepfather;

- I went through a painful divorce six years later;

- I broke my ankle (twice), ruptured my Achilles tendon and tore my patellar tendon;

- I received my master's degree from Temple University;

- I was first promoted to management;

- I let corporate America mess with my head, my heart, my spirit and my drive for 14 years;

- I had to drive to work two to three hours each way for three years;

- I spent the day in the hospital waiting for the results of my mother's brain aneurysm surgery;

- I remarried;

- my daughter Daecia was born;

- my best friend's brother, George, died suddenly at age 44 because of a brain aneurysm, leaving behind his wife and four daughters;

- my father died;

- I started using Jr. in my name;

- I started my own company, JIMPACT Enterprises;

- My second marriage failed;

My remembrances could go on, but I think you get the point. That's why my brother sends his friends my way. He believes I can relate to them and their situations, and help them land squarely on their feet. Though I have my own "stuff" to work through at times, I seldom turn down a potential "client" or an opportunity to help turn someone's rotten day around. I get that from my mother, too.

My friend Linda Gillette says she treats every day as a sparkling new adventure. Linda was born and raised in a small community in North Dakota. She says it was a great place to be raised but that magazines and TV stimulated much of her dreaming as a child. She says now, as an adult, her childhood dreams have become a reality. As a business day gets more and more stressful, she just smiles and thinks of where she came from. "Life is good; it is what it is," is one of her favorite quotes.

 Life without problems would be death. You know, you can only have good because of evil, sweet because of sour, etc.

Linda once told me, "We are all going to have hot and cold moments. It's good to embrace both temperatures. I read a book long ago by Norman Vincent Peale. He said a depressed man came up to him after he finished a speech and asked, 'How can I live my life with no problems?' Peale looked at the man and said, 'Die.' Well, the man didn't find the response humorous, but there is truth to the statement. Just understanding this helps me accept my world and in turn keeps me motivated." Linda is incredible!

I remember when my mother, brother and I moved out of our tiny, two-bedroom, one-bath, second floor apartment on Sansom Street to our first "real house," on Larchwood Avenue in Southwest Philadelphia. We were also moving away from my father. After 13 years of marriage, my mother had grown weary of the alcoholism, lying, disappointments, poor money management and abuse. We had kept the move a secret from him for fear that he would get violent or try to talk my mother out of leaving. We moved into our new, single-parent home while my dad was at work.

As an 11-year-old I didn't quite understand the risk my mother was taking. To me, we were just moving and Dad was not going with us. I thought my parents would eventually reunite—that Dad would find us and things would go back to the way they were, minus the alcohol. He said his affair with the bottle started as a way to warm his insides after spending each workday, as a butcher, working in frigid, freezer temperatures. He just never ended the relationship with liquor. Mom grew tired of his mistress. They never did get back together. My life story continued. My lessons mounted.

Our plot was now a single parent family. We were latchkey kids, two boys growing up in our first "house-house," a twin, row-house in our first interracial neighborhood. We lived right on the outskirts of the University of Pennsylvania's campus. I often saw college students of all nationalities going to class and going to parties. I loved this ethnic and racial diversity. Every day Mom rode public transportation to her job in Center City Philadelphia. And every Saturday, she woke up saying, "Jim, Rod get up…there's work to be done!"

We did not have all the material extras that many of our neighbors had. Other than our home, our 1975 white Chevy Nova was our most valuable asset and we bought that, our first car, when I was 16. I would use my creativity and resourcefulness to make bats, balls, baskets and bases from the strangest things in our basement and garage. Today you see basketball courts in the driveway; my brother and I used a puff basketball set to play full court in the dining room. Our foul line was a spot smack in the middle of the floor, directly across from the dining room cabinet doorknob.

We may have come up short in the "keep up with the Joneses race," but we did have a surplus of love. Mom, with the focus and concentration of a med-school student meticulously studying for final exams, was injecting into our lives the discipline, commitment, work ethic and responsibility that would last forever.

Like most kids growing up, I did get into my share of neighborhood fights. Those two-minute tussles were with friends who teased me whenever my mother decided to go out on a date. I guess, for the sake of my physical well-being, that it was a good thing Mom did not date too often. My friends had dads at home so they were rubbing it in that I did not have one or that I had, in their opinion, too many.

My interests on weekends and during the summer were few and simple: (1) eating TastyKakes, mustard pretzels and cherry water ices (my favorite snacks) and (2) playing sports outside and inside of the house with Rodney. Our living room and dining room became a multipurpose facility, quickly converted into a baseball field and basketball court while Mom was at work. We used a badminton racket as our bat and a puff basketball as our baseball. For bases we used old newspapers or couch pillows. Surprisingly, we never broke anything, except our individual records for points scored in an hour or before Mom got home.

Now, as a 43-year-old adult, I can say WOW! Mom was courageous. She left her husband during a time and era when it was extremely rare for a black woman to leave her marriage. Mom wanted a home, not just a house. She did not care that many of her other friends stayed in their trying marriages. She ignored the black-single-parent, single-woman stereotypes and labels. She had spirit. I often wonder if my mom's will to find happiness back then paved the way for my not being afraid to leave corporate jobs when I felt unfulfilled and unhappy.

Most people say that you need two incomes to raise a family. Nanci Smith did it extremely well with one. We never thought we were missing out on anything, save the occasional fashion statements and sneakers *du jour*. Mom was zeroing in on building our character and not going into poverty by spoiling us silly. Our summer vacations were a bus ride to my grandmother's house in South Philly—not to the shore or to a resort. We never missed school and Mom saw to it that our grades were always in honor roll range.

I believe that the discipline my mom instilled in me has played a role in my impatience with people who don't like to roll up their sleeves (and then make excuses or play the victim). Mom even went in to work the day after she officially retired (after 40 years of working for the City of Philadelphia). She said that she had several projects she had to wrap up.

Mom has handled her business superbly, always planting the seeds of life into our heads. As a child, the seeds took root inside both my head and my heart, never to be forgotten, and to be shared with so many others. The world, and most specifically our home, were our classrooms and our teacher lived with us. Other people and everyday experiences were our visual aids. I didn't have to take notes. The lessons were powerful and were repeated over and over again.

EXTRA AWESOME GIFT

I was raised in a household considered well below poverty level. My dad was a construction worker, but his hot temper often left the family with little money because he would lose his job frequently. Dad was an alcoholic. Mom, my six siblings and I often didn't see him for days at a time. We lived in a two-room house with no water, electricity or plumbing. Yes, we had an outhouse over the hill! It seemed nothing was stable in our lives except the love our parents gave us.

Growing up I often heard, "We don't have the money," and I learned as a child to begin to work for anything I needed or wanted.

I decided then that I was going to make it in this world and be the very best I could be. Although I wasn't blessed with wealth and material things, I inherited a big heart, love for all mankind and an outpouring of love for life.

I've encountered many bumps in the road during my life. I have overcome being a single parent with virtually no help from the children's father. I have battled a fight with cancer and won. My father came to live with me last year and I just recently lost him to cancer. Because I had to take care of my family during and after high school, I have not been able to finish college, but I have worked extremely hard and, with the help of many great people and mentors, I have built my confidence, matured professionally and made it up the ladder in the largest insurance company in the world. I am now an agent for this company.

I am so proud of my accomplishments! I'm proud of where I came from and I'm proud of where I've been and where I am going with my life! The greatest compliment that I receive is when people tell me that I am the most positive and strongest person they know.

Average: Occasionally reflecting on your past and how your past has played a role in who you are today.

Awesome: Vividly remembering those important lessons, making the appropriate life changes and teaching, coaching or mentoring others who could benefit from your life lessons.

Strength comes from perseverance and keeping a positive attitude. When you face challenges, keep a smile on your face, a prayer in your heart and a good attitude.

—*Tracie Johnson (Highland Heights, KY)*

Quickly turn to your Personal Awesome Action Plan Page (p. 233) and write the five "awesome actions" you're going to take as a result of reading this chapter. When you're finished, turn back to read more about what it takes to go from average to awesome!

GIFT

Savor Your Moments

*What I am beginning to learn at the age 48 is how to live
in the moment—how to pause...look about...as I walk to the bank,
drive my beautiful children to school, even as I put out the garbage
in the fresh early hours of the morning. I think about the incredible
natural and spiritual beauty that surrounds me.
I look, I feel, I appreciate and I'm thankful.*

—Judy Chapman (Toronto, Canada)

I started writing this chapter in my head in December 1981. I resumed writing it nearly 20 years later, in September 2001, as my wife (at the time), Pat, and I were driving to Pittsburgh to attend the wedding of my friends Becky and Nick.

Unlike many of the out-of-towners who attended the nuptials, we opted to drive to Pittsburgh from New Jersey rather than fly. As a motivational speaker, trainer and consultant, I'm a frequent flier and I see more airports than Disney World sees children during the summer time. So spending six hours in our car multi-tasking, playing catch-up with Pat, listening to Marvin Gaye and Tammi Terrell, Luther Vandross, Anita Baker, Regina Belle, Patti LaBelle, Babyface and Stevie Wonder, while preparing for an upcoming motivational workshop, appealed to me more than the prospect of facing long lines and privacy invading security checks at another airport.

I was in multi-tasking-mania as I drove, listening to *Babyface Unplugged*, searching deep inside my heart and mind for key motivational points to make during my upcoming speaking engagement. I wanted this program to rank as one of my best of all time, since I would be presenting it to a former employer. (You always want the ex to see you at your best.)

I continued to look out the window, admiring the effect the sun was having on the beautiful hillsides, searching for a clever way to capture the spirit of my favorite Benjamin E. Mays poem during my presentation:

"I have only just a minute,

only sixty seconds in it,

forced upon me—can't refuse it,

didn't seek it, didn't choose it.

But it's up to me to use it.

I must suffer if I lose it.

Give account if I abuse it.

Just a tiny little minute—

but eternity is in it."

I looked over to Pat and said, "I wish I had the camera." Our 35-millimeter was resting in the trunk with all of the other wedding stuff. I then got on my soapbox, "There are so many things that happen to us each day, so many moments, so many important times...we never spend time just capturing the moment or the feeling...we let the moment whisk right by. It's a shame! We rush through life!"

We need to savor our moments.

"We don't even honor the moments we have when we're talking one-on-one. There's always the cell phone, the pager or some other distraction competing for, and winning, our attention. We should take cameras with us all of the time so that we could always take pictures of our significant moments right away!"

Then it hit me! That was the point I was going to make! That was the point I was going to drive home during the session: to savor your moments! And, at that very moment, the words of Babyface glided from the car stereo, "…gone too soon."

I guess I developed this "savoring" sense when my mother, brother and I began our journey together alone without my Dad. We truly appreciated the times we had. Nanci and her two boys. We protected each other. We visited relatives together. We went to amusement parks together and we worked on and cleaned the house together. We had a number of deep family discussions. I loved those times!

Over twenty years ago, when I began writing this chapter in my head, I knelt in the middle of the field in Phenix City, Alabama, at the conclusion of the Amos Alonzo Stagg Bowl game (the National Championship for NCAA Division III football), which my team had won. I looked to the sky, feeling and listening to everything that was going on around me. The sun seemed to be singing, "CELEBRATE good times come on…" and my teammates were going crazy. They were hi-fiving, belly bumping and giving each other Gatorade show- ers. Our fans were also exuberant. I was the only one, several yards away, by myself silently reveling, processing, so in the moment. I wasn't being antisocial. I was savoring my moment.

Widener University had just beaten the University of Dayton 17- 10 for the Division III National Football Championship. I would get a championship ring, celebrations back on campus, an all-night, floor shaking party at the tiny Black Student Union house and a life lesson that I would recall 20 years later.

I don't know what motivated me not to immediately join in on all the on-field frivolity at the time. Maybe I was thinking about the two playoff losses that had ended our seasons during my freshman and sophomore years. Maybe I was thinking of our mind-numbing 28—

24 loss to Dayton (we were winning 24—0 at halftime) in the play-offs the previous season. Maybe I was thinking about the hundreds of thousands of college athletes, male and female, who never win a national championship. Maybe I was thinking about the fact that I would be the first student/athlete from my high school, University City, to ever win a college championship. Maybe I was thinking about the National Championship ring that I was going to wear for the rest of my life. Maybe I was thinking that this would be as close as I'd ever come to playing in the Super Bowl. Or maybe I was just thinking about the magnitude of our accomplishment, especially since we had been losing 10-0 at halftime. I think the answer is all of the above.

I remember exactly what I was feeling as I looked at the grass, looked at the people jumping around, looked at the dejected faces of the Dayton players and fans, and looked to my God to thank him for everything he'd done for me. I eventually joined the on-field hysteria, but for those first few minutes, I was having a moment…savoring my special moment…a moment that I will never forget.

How are you doing right now in savoring your moments?

We live and work in a society where we are always in a hurry. We rush as we get dressed in the morning. We rush to work. We rush to meetings. We rush to the bathroom. We rush home and we rush our dinner down our throats. We rush conversations with friends and loved ones. We rush to get promoted and we rush to judgment. Have you ever wanted someone to just cut to the chase rather than providing you with all of the supporting details?

I can recall my first promotion to management in corporate America. I had been counting the days. According to my personal Jim Smith file, I did what I thought I needed to do. I had my Bachelor's degree (and was working on my Master's), put in my time, paid my dues, moved laterally to position myself for promotion and worked extremely diligently for six very taxing, but beneficial, years. Each year had seemed like a decade whenever one of my department colleagues, the friends with whom I had joined the organization and who had been my teammates in inter-company sports leagues, was promoted. What a bittersweet taste! Of course I was thrilled for them—we ate lunch together every day; we played fantasy football together; we were like a family during and after work. But, at the same time, I was miffed. For some reason that was never clearly explained to me, my corporate ladder just seemed steeper, more slippery and more difficult to climb than theirs. We were all bright, all professional, all personable and all diligent and competent workers. We even partnered on many projects. There was one major difference however: our race. I did not want to believe that race played a factor. I just wanted, yet never received, a thorough explanation. I kept asking management for clarification. I wanted to win, not wilt.

I was the next to the last of our "work family" to get promoted to management. The last to join the management ranks was my buddy Skip. Skip's black too.

When my boss first made the announcement during a quickly called division meeting, handing me the promotion envelope with everyone anxiously standing outside of her office, I thanked her and quickly excused myself from the celebration. I retreated to my own office to savor my moment. I had a private celebration filled with tears and prayers. I thought to myself, "I did it! I did it! Finally, I did it!"

As word of my promotion spread, a phenomenon occurred that made this promotion even more special: I was treated like some sort of a messiah by many of the other blacks in the organization. I felt like I was Dr. Martin Luther King, Jr., Muhammad Ali, Tom Joyner and Tavis Smiley rolled into one when, as I walked through the halls, I was greeted with an enthusiastic "thank you" or "don't forget me" or "about time they promoted one of us to management."

Peter Dailey, one of my mentors at the time, took me to lunch to celebrate my promotion. Peter was class personified: brilliant, funny, clever, soft-spoken and well dressed. I loved watching him with people. I asked him to be my mentor initially because my other mentor, Sylvia Garvin, a black woman, told me that if I wanted to learn many of the tricks of the game called corporate America, I would need a white male mentor. She believed that white males had influence, information and with that, the power. Peter was white.

Although I wish that I had first asked Peter to be my mentor because I thought he was the best person for the job and because I marveled at how he carried himself, rather than using his race as the most determining factor, I benefited from his wisdom and thoroughness nonetheless. During our mentoring relationship, Peter and I learned plenty about each other.

However, I would shortly learn something else that would completely blow me away. Sylvia provided that lesson too. She told me that Peter wasn't white enough. "What's white enough?" I thought. She believed Peter, who was also a member of the organization's professional affinity group for minorities, was blacker than many of the other black people in the company (i.e., he had a lot of soul in his stroll, his approach to life and in his spirit). She encouraged me to maintain my relationship with Peter, but said that if I was truly serious about spreading my corporate wings, I would need mentoring from a seasoned white male leader, who was sharp, tough, aggressive, rigid, old-fashioned, averse to the corporate love affair that organizations had with diversity initiatives and who had exclusive membership in the "good old boys'" club. She believed that this type of mentor, who arguably would be difficult to enlist, could help open the club doors that seemed cemented, bolted and padlocked shut to me before. I did find such mentors, more doors were opened, but that's another story, for another day, perhaps my next book.

During my promotion-celebration lunch, Peter reminded me of the significance of savoring your moments. He told me to always remember how I felt right at that very moment. He said the feeling would help me during times when I needed a pick-me-up. Because of Peter, I save thank-you notes and cards that people send me, and I also record and save the thank-you voice mails that I receive. I've become a moment-savoring machine. Peter also pushed my reward-yourself snowball down the hill. I talk about that more in Chapter 26. Thank you, Peter. File, save.

We really should take a camera along, figuratively or literally, everywhere we go. How many times have you heard someone say, "Man, I wish I had my camera!"? Sure, we have our cameras poised and ready during graduations, holidays, anniversaries, births and family reunions. But is that it? Are those the only times where we create or have wonderful memories?

What moments have you had today? How about this month? This year? December 31st is not the only time for personal reflection!

Not too long ago, I was having a rather poignant conversation with my good friend, Aileen. We were talking about making the most of one's time and she began to tell me about "that lady on the plane." My interest was piqued, and I asked her to continue with her story.

Aileen said that she was flying home after a business trip and brief visit with some old friends. She said she was feeling disappointed that the visit was so brief, that her friends, who she had not seen for some time, were super busy and couldn't spend the time together that they had anticipated. She said the woman sitting next to her picked up on Aileen's melancholy mood and asked what was wrong. Aileen briefly told her what was troubling her but was surprised and forever changed with "the lady's" response.

"The lady on the plane" said that she had just finished visiting her daughter, who was in the military. She explained that her daughter had scheduled that particular week off so that they could spend quality time together; they only saw each other twice a year. The lady said that she had eagerly flown out to Los Angeles only to find out, upon her arrival, that her daughter had been called to work. Aileen said how sorry she was to hear that the lady's vacation had been ruined. In response the lady said, "It wasn't ruined…although the time we had was limited, I was happy just being in LA, knowing that when my daughter came home from work, I would be there. Just to know that I was sharing her space for one week was enough for me."

Through her anecdote the lady told Aileen that she savored her moments with her daughter. She said that they laugh, smile and make the most of every moment they have together.

Aileen absorbed the lesson and vowed to change her perspective. Humbly and candidly she acknowledged that it wasn't going to be easy but that she was going to do it. She said that going forward she was going to tell all of her friends, and other special ones in her life, how great it was to see them, to be with them… how much richer her life is as a result of knowing them. "The lady on the plane"—a person, a moment my friend will savor for a long time.

My friend Laura Bruner earned her certification in "moment-savoring" last year. She recently shared with me the experience that changed her forever. "Jim, last year I survived an automobile accident that changed my approach to life," she began. "My little sports car and three other cars were totaled in the crash. As I careened into oncoming highway traffic, I quietly closed my eyes because I believed I was living my last moments on earth. Fortunately, however, when I opened my eyes I realized rescue workers would soon have me out of my crushed car and on the way to the emergency room. I did get pretty banged up, but I lived. I have stopped throwing the present away. I treasure life and make sure I send lots of thank you notes!"

As I put the bow on this chapter I couldn't help but think of the many moments that have shaped my life. They have taken permanent residence in my mind. I can't wait to have more. I'll savor them too. *How are you doing right now in savoring your moments?*

Average: Remembering to take your physical camera along to capture special moments on holidays and special occasions.

Awesome: Routinely taking your mental and physical camera along to capture your special, significant, planned and unplanned moments. Sharing your moments with others. Keeping a daily journal, even if it's just a few lines, to keep the memories alive. Saving voicemails from your favorite people. Not being in a hurry!

EXTRA AWESOME GIFT

Being mostly an "up" person, I believe I remain that way by enjoying the people around me, actually the world around me. I wake up every day happy to be given another day to surround myself with beautiful scenery and people I love and care about. Keeping a positive attitude seems to draw and inspire positive results. Sure, there are down times, but during those times, I always think to myself, "this too shall pass." That little phrase has gotten me through many rough periods by helping me to remember that other "down" times passed, and in an entire lifetime, only lasted for a very short time before all was well again.

—Barb Kompelein (Edina, MN)

Quickly turn to your Personal Awesome Action Plan Page (p. 233) and write the five "awesome actions" you're going to take as a result of reading this chapter. When you're finished, turn back to read more about what it takes to go from average to awesome!

3
GIFT

Remember Your Titans

Awesome comes from my having a family, mentors, co-workers and cheerleaders who are supportive and who demonstrate that success doesn't have to mean sacrifice. They applaud my wins and nudge me back into the game after a defeat.

—Sheryl B. Craun (Salem, NH)

I'm not the average moviegoer. I don't attend premieres and I love standing in long lines about as much I'd enjoy drinking a 32-ounce jar of that hot, yellow, Chinese mustard. Lately, the only movies I've gone to see, thanks to my daughter Daecia, have had a Disney flavor: *Shrek (I and II); Peter Pan; Fat Albert; The Incredibles; and A Shark's Tale.* In fact, with my busy schedule, I usually wait for movies to make it to cable. There, without the interruptions of boisterous laughs and people standing to make bathroom, Raisinettes and popcorn runs, I can comfortably watch the movies from my couch. However, a couple of years ago I saw a movie that will go into my top five movies of all time.

On a flight from Philadelphia to Phoenix, I was very pleasantly surprised, intrigued and uplifted by the movie selected. I was treated to *Remember the Titans*. If you haven't seen it, rent it. Then buy it! Fast!

When the movie first came out in theaters, I didn't break my neck or my schedule to go to see it. Typical Disney sports movie, I thought. The for-children-only movie, I believed, would have a little drama, provoke a few tears, then conclude with a happy ending. There would be happy good guys and happy bad guys, happy pets, happy music and happy credits. Maybe some pixie dust and animation? Boy, was I wrong. I was moved, touched, changed and reminded. I cried. I laughed. I remembered. I sat motionless at the end.

Titans, a true story, quickly took me back to my youth, my years of playing Little League football for YGS (Young Great Society), for University City High School in West Philadelphia and for Widener University in college.

In this true story, Denzel Washington plays Herman Boone, an embattled, drill-sergeant tough, black football coach in a 1971 racially divided neighborhood, school district and football program. The T. C. Williams High School Titans are his black and white student-athletes who learn, through Boone and his white assistant head coach, Bill Yost (played by Will Patton), about football execution, building relationships, team chemistry, racial inequities, teamwork and love. During these tough-love, no-pain-no-gain moments, Boone has to contend with the white town folks who want him ousted as head coach and the white referees who collude in attempts to steal the Titans' moral and on-field victories.

Boone's minefields also include building a relationship with Yost, a popular, respected and legendary town favorite who had been the team's head coach before equal opportunity legislation led to Boone's replacing him. Before the movie concludes, they all come together, save some of the neighborhood folks, to form an impenetrable bond.

Who are your Titans? Who are the people who always have your best interests at the forefront of their minds? Who are the people who always have your back? Who are the people who call you just to say they care? Who are the people who have left indelible marks on your life? Who are the people that love you in spite of the fact that you talk with food in your mouth or that you never return their calls in a timely manner?

Do your Titans mean a great deal to you? Really? If so, then why don't you check in with them more often? Why don't you drop them a line to let them know that you care? Why don't you send them more thank-you notes? It's one of the mysteries in life that we always name streets or buildings after people once they have passed away.

My Titans have played pivotal roles in both my personal and professional lives. Descriptions? Just think diversity.

As a teenager, and then as a college student, I formed a team of Titans comprised of mostly athletic coaches. Because my parents were divorced and I did not have a consistent father figure in my life, I really latched onto the men who led my athletic teams. Only one of those men was black (Mr. Sam); most of my Titans/coaches/dads (they were one and the same) were Jewish men, namely Sonny Elia (my high school junior varsity baseball and basketball coach) and Steve Kane (my high school varsity basketball coach).

We had, and still have, AWESOME relationships. I can still recall during my freshman and sophomore years in college telephoning Steve from my dormitory, fuming about how I thought the football coaches were treating me unfairly. Ironically, after my final year on the team, one of those coaches apologized to me for not playing me more, sooner. Imagine my white Titan/coach/dad doing his best to console me and offer solutions for my deep beliefs that favoritism and racism were also opponents I had to tackle.

Another one of my Titans, my great grandmother Carrie Bryant, recently passed away at the age of 97. She practically raised me during my early teenage years when I spent many of my summers at her three-story, South Philadelphia home. She used to wear me out in checkers and in pinochle. Grandmom is my heart. I remember all of the times we played checkers for pennies and she cleaned my clock. She would win every one of my tired little pennies. The routine was the same. She would crush me in penny checkers. I would fight back tears, then head down the third floor steps back to the first floor. Before I got too far, she would call me back, give me back my pennies and tell me to practice up before I challenged her again. That was Grandmom.

She taught me about responsibility, commitment, caring and personal empowerment. Some of my favorite memories from those summers include playing hide and go seek, basketball, half-ball, dead-block, tops, riding my bike and doing chores for "Grams." I really enjoyed washing dishes because Grams loved a clean kitchen. For over 50 years she traveled up and down the three stories with one single objective—put out the family fires on the first and second floors that threatened to pull our dysfunctional family further apart.

During our wedding reception ten years ago, my ex-wife and I made sure we selected an extra long song (Taylor Dayne's extended version of *I'll Always Love You* was the choice) during the family introductions. We wanted to make sure Grandmom had sufficient time to walk down the aisle to her seat so that everyone could see and marvel at the woman, and feel the strength that had enabled her to keep our family together. Prior to the wedding, I kept asking her if she was going to be there. She would just calmly smile and say, "God willing Jimmy, I'll be there." She was an incredible Titan!

Kathy Cook was my manager for three years at one of my corporate stops. The five-foot, fast-walking and fast-talking, charismatic woman taught me more about professionalism in the three years I reported to her than I had learned in the previous nine. She always provided the appropriate feedback (a timely anecdote, coaching conversation, hug, handshake or slap on the wrist). She was savvy. She was strategic. She was tough. She was brilliant. She knew how to manage and how to motivate people. She taught me about not taking on bad business.

I remember wanting to help lead our organization's diversity initiative upon coming on board. Kathy had hired me to coach, develop and train supervisors and managers. Since I had done an enormous amount of diversity work at my previous job I thought this would be a sensational way to make an immediate impact at the company.

Kathy said "ABSOLUTELY NOT!" She said, "Jim, there will be time later for you to do diversity work here. I want people to get to know you as a person and to see your management development abilities and talents…not just see another black man leading another diversity council. I don't want them to avoid you. I want them to embrace you. I want you to build allies."

I did not realize it right away, but like my mother's protective lesson about always appearing approachable and smiling, Kathy's plan seemed to me to be strategic and protective, but somehow unfair. I remember thinking, "What kind of world are we living in when a manager believes she has to divert an employee's interest to another assignment because of the stereotypes, beliefs, attitudes and mindsets that go along with being a person of color heading up a particular position?"

Consider the loss. The company lost a valuable diversity resource. I lost a valuable opportunity to assist the organization by utilizing my diversity skills, resources, experiences and talents—all in the name of perceived bias and prejudices.

At any rate, three years and an Award of Excellence later, Kathy asked me if I was ready to get back into the diversity business. I had built a solid track record and there were plenty of opportunities brewing with my name written on many of them. I declined any large role. I told her that if we could connect the diversity responsibilities within my new role as an Organizational Effectiveness Consultant, I would do it. And we did—successfully. Consider my gain.

I left the organization shortly after that. During my surprise going-away party (of course Kathy orchestrated the entire event), I was exuberant, yet torn. I loved what my new job offered but I would be leaving my coach, my boss, my mentor, my Titan and my friend, Kathy Cook. As the silverware began to clink the glasses, and choruses of "speech, speech, speech" began to mount, I walked to the front of the room. With Kathy at my side I began to thank everyone for being awesome colleagues and teammates. When I began to thank Kathy, I turned to look at my Titan, and it was sob city. During my "the way we were speech," I cried like a toddler whose favorite ball had just rolled into the sewer.

Question. Do you routinely take your Titans for granted? What's that about? I am where I am today because of my Titans.

 We spend more time with our Titanics, the people who bring us down and intentionally or unintentionally try to sink us, than we do with our Titans. Why?

Titans are consistent and more dependable than the person who delivers your mail. They help you to give birth to your greatness or rediscover it. Through their words and their actions, they provide immeasurable support. Just when you're feeling drained from drama or whipped from worry, they give you a call out of the blue or send you a note to remind you how important you are to them. So call them more often. Visit them more often. E-mail them more often. Remember your Titans!

EXTRA AWESOME GIFT

I would not be where I am today without the unconditional love and support of my soulmate, my best friend, my husband. His continual belief in my talents has helped me to make the sacrifice I may not have wanted to make, but which ultimately paid off for me, personally and professionally. His willingness to keep the home fires burning and spend many days alone while I have been on the road is what has helped me face those countless nights in Holiday Inns. I know that he will always be there for me, encouraging, listening, laughing and holding me. His eagerness to be both mom and dad when needed is what has helped me be anything but average. He always thinks I am awesome, even when I don't feel like it.

—Priscilla Shumway (Island of the Palms, SC)

Quickly turn to your Personal Awesome Action Plan Page (p. 233) and write the five "awesome actions" you're going to take as a result of reading this chapter. When you're finished, turn back to read more about what it takes to go from average to awesome!

GIFT

Get Mad, Get Sad, Get Better, Get Busy

I won't allow myself to regress to past failures unless it is to analyze
how I could have done them differently or better.
I live each day to the fullest.
I'd rather burn out than rust out.
Life is too short to spend it complaining.
I enjoy living!

—*Roberta Salisbury (Hinckley, ME)*

Have you ever had a pity party? Come on. You know, those parties where you sit around moaning and groaning, heaving and grieving, crying and complaining, whining and worrying about some misfortune that has happened to you—and then not doing anything about it. I've had my share!

Being raised in a single parent family did not trigger them, however, nor did my family's lack of money and lack of material wealth. I was challenged and at times frustrated, yet strengthened, time after time when I attended mostly white schools. I got used to being the only black person. Those realities were character-building and developmental; they prepared me for the real world.

I guess what did prompt my first significant party was the unexpected moment when Benae, my high school sweetheart (and fiancée), abruptly ended our relationship shortly after I graduated from college. To say I was devastated is an understatement.

We started dating when we were in high school. I was a senior and she was a junior. I was captain of the football, baseball and basketball teams and she was captain of the cheerleading squad. Everyone in our circle of friends believed that Smitty and Nay were going to be together until death did we part. We often kidded each other about designing the interior of our home using our black and gold high school colors.

Benae even joined me at Widener for college. She left after two years to finish school in Philadelphia, but our relationship continued to flourish. We got engaged during the second semester of my senior year. Our relationship was the stuff Paramount and Columbia Pictures crave—except that our ending was as unexpected and as sudden as Magic Johnson's initial announcement that he was retiring from playing professional basketball for the Los Angeles Lakers because he was HIV-positive.

Shortly after I graduated from college, Benae said (and I'm sure that I'm not the only male who abhors this phrase), "This isn't working for me, but we can still be friends." She said that she wanted to grow and to start seeing other people; and that if we were meant to be, we would get together again at some point. I was crushed. My fairy tale relationship was over. The football player and the cheerleader was now a painful memory. For the rest of the summer and right through the fall, I had one long, exasperating, pity party. Every song on the radio, every show on television and every movie I went to see to take my mind off Benae reminded me of our yesterdays.

After that, the parties started to occur more often than reruns on Nick At Nite. One would think I was a pity party animal.

During the Benae pity party, other parties started occuring simultaneously. The music became deafening. The USFL Philadelphia Stars cut me—and my professional football hopes—three months after the Benae break-up. Sitting in the stands teary-eyed, knowing that I would never again hear the crowd's roar or that I would never feel the rush of adrenaline that competitive sport creates, was a tough pill to swallow. In addition, I had ongoing gainful unemployment mini-pity-parties after months of unsuccessfully trying to turn my English degree into a career.

Actually, my ongoing Benae pity parties affected me more than I realized. I got married by a Justice of the Peace eight months after Benae and I went our separate ways. I had known my wife for just four months, having met her at a friend's wedding on New Year's Eve, 1983. We exchanged our vows four months later on April 28, 1984. I also became her four-year-old son's stepfather. My rationale: I went from not having anyone to love to now having two people to wrap my arms around. Our union lasted six maturing, tumultuous and character-building years.

Coincidentally, Benae married four months after I did. I'm certain I saw her wedding party drive by my home as I sat on my front porch that August afternoon. Seeing them took me back to the "we can just be friends" break-up day. Ouch!

During my early corporate America years, I had a pity party nearly every time someone in my department whom I deemed less deserving received a promotion instead of me. I wasn't used to being bypassed. It was humbling and frustrating. I can't say that I ever got used to it. My ex-wife would always say, "…then do something about it!" In fact, that *was* my modus operandi for every other challenge in my life, but this was different. This felt more paralyzing. So whenever I believed I was encountering institutional racism, classism, nepotism, bias, stereotypes, and the like, if you brought the music, I would bring the resentment, the rage and the resistance. If I wasn't partying alone, I hosted pity parties with other mournful partygoers.

Our pity parties had a familiar routine—share your dilemma, get agreement that it wasn't your fault, share what you were or were not going to do as a result, then close your remarks with, "see…that's why it doesn't make a difference if you…" Some of those parties were classic. We all ordered all we could from that "whine list of life."

I remember when I worked for my first major company and my good friend Skip and I would sit in my car after work for hours, pity partying about yet another white guy from our inner circle of friends who had gotten a promotion over us. Ironically, it always rained on those days. I can still see the windshield wipers slowly going back and forth, back and forth, and back and forth. They made a quirky noise. Rather than hearing squish, squish, squish, squish, I heard, as the wipers went back and forth, "left out again, left out again, left out again." Skip and I felt helpless and we were livid. At times I wanted to put my fist through the window. At times I wanted to quit. I didn't care that I did not have another job to go to.

We also moved into depression. After questioning ourselves, our work habits and our performance, we took dead aim at the organization. I always woke up from those pity parties with horrible, "I still work there," hangovers. Trying to come up with personal solutions for systemic problems was gut-wrenching.

My other hangovers were the aftermath of dwelling on no-win issues like, "why me?" or "what could have/should have been" or "it hurts so much." I was always an over-achiever. I wanted the A-plus. I was in the National Honor Society in high school. I was a captain on every athletic team, every level, that I played for. I more than held my own in spite of the racial imbalances of several of my schools. I was accustomed to shaking off the dust and getting back up. I welcomed and weathered the storms. Nothing could break my spirit. But, for the first five or six years after college graduation, I wavered. Two failed relationships and corporate "play-with-your-head" games really rocked my personal belief system.

During my divorce, I had an epiphany: Sometimes life isn't hard—we make it hard. Sure, life isn't always going to be a picturesque day in Aruba, but it's what you do after you get the run in your pantyhose, the shopping cart in the back of the ankle or the empty gas tank in the middle of nowhere, that counts.

Pity parties only linger if you let them linger. I cannot say what the exact trigger was, but sometime in the midst of all of my divorce muck, I decided that going forward, when things looked bleak, I would get mad, get sad, get better and then get busy. I felt empowered! I still feel empowered!

Please don't think I'm insensitive. I do understand that life is painful sometimes. Unforeseen circumstances seemingly occur as often as creditor calls. The sting of a loved one's death can last for what seems like forever. And yes, sometimes you have to have that sorrowful, "it-hurts-all-over" cry. But with time, we have to move on. Learn from the experience, file, save it, but move on. Burn the negative tapes. Turn off the pity party soundtracks. Turn on the full-steam-ahead adrenaline. Soren Kirkegaard said,

 "Life can only be understood backwards, but it must be lived forwards."

My friend Tony Spann has been like a second brother since we met in second grade at the Henry C. Lee Elementary School's little red schoolhouse in 1967. With the last names "Smith" and "Spann," we sat next to each other in many of our classes during that memorable year and those that followed. My family became his extended family and vice versa. His oldest brother, George, filled in as my "voice of wisdom" and "big brother" during my teenage and early adult years.

When Tony saw his mother's phone number on his pager late one evening at his Chicago home, he had a sinking feeling that she hadn't called just for a trivial chat or a routine check-in. He sensed that something terrible had occurred. When he returned the call, he braced himself, but not adequately.

George had died.

"Never in my wildest dreams did I think my mother's news would be so devastating," Tony would tell me. "I found myself experiencing feelings that I had never experienced before. I found myself enraged, bewildered, depressed, deeply saddened and overwhelmed by grief. George was my brother and my confidant, as well as my father figure.

Losing him was catastrophic for me. I was numb for days. Simultaneously, as if functioning in two parallel universes, I became inspired to get my family through this depressing period of our collective lives. I began to see things in a different, clearer light. I was instrumental in consoling everyone, and my immediate focus switched to playing a significant role in all of our family matters leading up to the day of his funeral and for the first two years after his death. I never actually gave myself the opportunity to grieve until I felt that everyone in my immediate family, as well as his widow and four daughters, had reached a point where they could function relatively 'normally' under the circumstances. His memory and spirit were guiding me, motivating me to provide emotional, financial and physical support to everyone. The other amazing thing that occurred was that I became acutely aware of my mortality.

"This realization moved me to pursue everything with renewed vigor and dedication. I felt invincible; it was as if all of George's skills, abilities and talents had merged with mine. My desire to enrich my family members' lives in every possible way became my preoccupation. I talked about him in the present tense and I shared every memory I had with anyone who would listen.

"James, as a result of George's death," Tony continued, "I believe that I am more complete; my confidence is as high as ever and I believe that I can and will achieve anything my heart desires. He is still my inspiration; his memory helps me to keep things in perspective. I feel like the Phoenix, coming out of the ashes, as if reborn, to live a self-fulfilling prophecy."

I know a number of individuals who have given in to life's inequities and kicks in the teeth. They have timeshares in Victimville. Their perception of the world never changes. Their perception of themselves never changes. Their favorite quote is, "If it is to be, don't look at me." As a result, I've come to believe that we get what we expect, not what we want. We get what we are. Our external world is significantly impacted by our internal world. Consequently, when we expect negative things are going to happen, because negative thoughts are running recklessly through our minds, they usually do.

It's easy to throw a pity party. It's easy to wallow in, "Oh well, I can't do anything about it." It's easy to blame the system or blame the loss. Remember that awesome people, in the throes of drama, pain, unfairness and uncertainty, get mad, get sad, get better, and then get busy. Today, Tony is doing incredibly well. He is still on a mission. George's memory is his bridge to greatness, not his roadblock. When George died, Tony got mad, got sad, then eventually got better. And he stays busy, consistently striving toward awesome.

> **Average:** Holding on to negative feelings and letting those negative feelings affect the decisions you make.

> **Awesome:** Learning from unfortunate situations and occurrences and letting those times become catalysts for continued personal growth, desire, development, discipline, determination, and strength.

⭐ EXTRA AWESOME GIFT

My mom once told me (and she had an extremely difficult time as a single parent raising my brother and me), "What other choice do I have—to be negative? How would that help me with all that I have on my plate? It serves no purpose!" Those words stay with me when I start to think or speak negatively. We all have to vent our frustrations at times, and sometimes just the release will help you get past the negative feelings, allowing you to focus on the positive. My motto is: release it, and then move on! Don't ignore it, or it will resurface. Purge it. Do whatever it takes, but make sure it's gone!

—Lisa Marzullo (Chicago, IL)

Quickly turn to your Personal Awesome Action Plan Page (p. 234) and write the five "awesome actions" you're going to take as a result of reading this chapter. When you're finished, turn back to read more about what it takes to go from average to awesome!

GIFT

Ready, Aim, Fire Up an Awesome Day!

I have regular practices that help me generate positive energy.
I meditate, exercise, journal, read and write a "grateful list" every day.
—*Deloris Davis (Philadelphia, PA)*

My cubicle in the office building was directly adjacent to a massive, long, tinted window overlooking the employee parking lot. The window reminded me of one that you would look through to observe sea life at the Camden or Baltimore aquarium. Since the window was tinted, it gave me a private, early-morning view of my coworkers' daily regimens—slowly emerging from their cars, reluctantly trudging to their nine-to-fives. They usually appeared somber, fatigued, frustrated, wearing sour expressions.

Once inside, some of them, with attitudes to match their facial expressions, would stagger to the cafeteria to satisfy their morning coffee addiction and hunger pangs. My typically "good morning" greetings were usually met with: "What's so good about it?" "Don't talk to me until I get my coffee!" "Jim, what are you so happy about...people like you really annoy me." "You know I'm not a morning person... I'll call you later."

These people were doing their Johnnie Cochran best to argue for an absolutely pitiful morning. They would object to any motions for smiles and laughter. And they were successful, winning their "bad morning" cases day after day, day after day.

How do you start each day?

The morning is an opportune time for programming your subconscious—it's most alert and open to new information at this point.

Before you get out of bed what do you think about? A dead-end job? A stressful relationship? A two-hour commute? An irritating manager or team leader? Suppose you made time to contemplate your upcoming day before you headed to the bathroom each morning. If there was a daily-life menu sitting on your lap, offering a variety of items that represented the type of day you could have, what would you see? Imagine that the menu had two pages, a page of entrees on the left and a page of entrees on the right. The page on the left represents entrees that could create an average day and the page on the right represents awesome-day entrees.

Would your entrees be limited to just a few items? How much would they vary? Any specials? Would your subconscious tell you that you were out of AWESOME entrees? Knowingly or unknowingly, consciously or unconsciously, we choose entrees that represent the kind of day we're probably going to have. The disappointing reality is that most people go straight to the AVERAGE side. And they order and eat the same stuff everyday. Do you ever hear people, when asked how their day is going, say, "same old stuff?" Well, who's at fault?

The picture that comes to my mind in this case is of someone slowly rising up while sitting on the edge of the bed. He/she wipes the sleep and crust from his/her eyes and reaches down toward the floor. But rather than reaching for a comfortable pair of slippers he/she hungrily reaches for his/her daily menu and opens it up to the AVERAGE choices. Thinking to an imaginary waiter he/she says:

> *"I'll take the usual. For breakfast I'd like to have one of those 'didn't hear my alarm and overslept' and a 'get stuck in traffic on the way to work.' I'll take a side order of that 'coffee stain on my tie' and give me a little helping of that 'burn my forehead with my curling iron' and the 'cafeteria closes as soon as I get there for my morning*

coffee.' For lunch I'll take a big helping of that 'my boss is getting on my nerves.' I wonder how that 'my computer shuts down' will taste. Anyway, I'll take a side of those 'long, waste-of-time meetings where nothing gets accomplished.' To drink, give me a 'coffee burns my tongue.' For dinner, you have to give me one of those 'another late night at the office.' For my two dinner sides, I'll take the 'someone got the credit for one of my ideas' and the 'no change for the toll-booth.' Dessert? I'll take 'a flat tire' and 'a splitting headache.'"

The vision I see for someone choosing from the AWESOME entrees is significantly different:

"For breakfast I'd like a slice of that 'awesome morning work-out,' 'a healthy, filling meal before I get into the office' and a 'read at least 10 pages of my favorite book.' I'll also take a side of 'one of my all time favorite songs is playing while I drive in.' For lunch I'd like to have a huge order of that 'quick but meaningful in-and-out of the daycare for toddler drop-offs or pick-ups' and one of those 'the time just flies by as I zoom through my morning.' I'd also like a bowl of that 'helping a coworker through a difficult decision.' For dinner, I'd like, but it must be well done, 'an extremely productive day at the job I love.' I'd also like, for one of my two sides, a 'compliment from a coworker on a job well done on one of my projects,' and for the other side order, 'a high five from one of the facilities workers as I leave the building.' For dessert, just give me a big helping of a 'dinner with the people I love the most' and 'a great night of rest.'"

We do have an enormous amount of power to determine what kind of day we're going to have.

But it doesn't stop there. When it comes to determining what clothes you're going to wear each day, do you choose clothes from the average side of the closet or the awesome side? The average side of the closet offers clothes that you just throw on. You don't feel particularly powerful or motivated in these clothes. Yes, they match and they fit (for the most part). But they're not the colors or the patterns or the cuts that make you feel or appear awesome and empowered.

The awesome side of the closet offers clothes that help you to feel powerful. They fit you extremely well, all over. The colors bring out your smile and your natural energy. They highlight or accent your best features. They're clothes that add an additional pep to your step, groove to your move and glide to your stride. People usually comment on how good you look and as a result your attitude and performance reflect how awesome you feel.

Unfortunately, many of us, because we're usually running late or we're tired, just reach into the average side of the closet and just pull out the first thing we put our hands on. This is often the set-up for an incredibly, predictable, average day.

My friend Leann Bohn told me about a morning that recently tested her morning average-vs.-awesome selection process. "Last night my daughter, for some reason, couldn't go to sleep until after 11:00 PM," she began. "My son was awakened not much later by severe abdominal pains, which required a trip to the emergency room. Turned out that he had strep throat, not appendicitis. The fog was so thick on the drive back from the emergency room at 5:00 in the morning that I could hardly see. And on the way into work, the traffic was unusually heavy due to the torrential rainfall. At one point I had to slam on the brakes, causing the entire contents of my purse to spill out all over the floor of my car. When I finally got into work, I had so much to carry that my arms were full and I couldn't carry an umbrella. I arrived five minutes late, dripping wet. BUT all I kept saying to myself was, 'The AWESOME side of the menu, Leann, choose from the AWESOME side.' The rest of my day was pretty good after that. And as for the rain, I really didn't mind not having an umbrella. I'm beginning to appreciate just how great rain really feels."

Each day we have the power to have an average day or an awesome day. What do you choose?

I'm reminded of a job I had that required a two-hour commute each way. During my second month with the company there was a terrible ice storm. I left work early, thinking that my long commute might take twice as long as usual. I stopped to fill the tank with gas and get a few snacks in case I got stuck. Sure enough, as soon as I merged onto the main highway I did get stuck.

So I listened to the radio, read the newspaper and ate cherry Twizzlers while waiting for the traffic to move. I began to ration my Twizzlers when I realized I would be spending much of the night in my car on the highway with hundreds of other frustrated motorists. Impatient drivers skidded off the road into the embankment or unsuccessfully tried to maneuver across the embankment to exit the highway. "In a hurry to get stuck," I thought to myself as I continued my game plan of half a Twizzler every half-hour.

I finally reached home at 3:30 AM. My car died and I ended up taking the rest of the week off to recover and to get my car repaired.

Thoughts of finding a new job danced through my head for a minute. No job is worth this everyday aggravation. But then I turned the pity party music off. Working for this company was the chance of a lifetime. I had connected with both my manager and my vice president and I was not going to let my long commute dampen my spirits.

So every morning before I headed to the car, rather than thinking about the stop-and-go parking lot traffic I was bound to face, I thought about what CDs I was going to listen to. My car also became a virtual library for learning. I listened to motivational and educational tapes and did an awful lot of thinking, designing and creating. I began to look forward to the commute, welcoming the opportunity to play personal, self-reflective catch-up. I spent the equivalent of one entire day in my car commuting each week.

In spite of my arduous drive, I still ordered AWESOME entrees from the menu. I was going to be all right. I was making a huge difference for my department and for the organization. I had developed an awesome reputation for supervisor and management development and I loved my job. I even began doing my first in-house motivational presentations while there. What a training ground!

This enriching experience would soon come to an end, though. The commute and my newborn daughter, Daecia, ultimately caused my exodus. Because of my departure time in the morning and my return time in the evening, whenever I saw my little angel during the week she was asleep or waking me up at some ungodly hour in the morning full of tears. Moving was not an option because we had only been in our new "dream home" for less than a year. I would soon secure another job a lot closer to home. I had to spend more quality time with Daecia.

I think it's a given: for an awesome day don't even consider the average entrees or the average side of the closet. Eat right! Dress right! And don't waver. Don't let other people's average mornings change your positive outlooks and perspectives. I once had a manager who would storm into the office some days. Nearly everyone else in the department would walk around on eggshells, not wanting to appear happy. Not me! I had already had an awesome morning before I got into the office.

I guess I'm greedy. I start thinking about my awesome entrees the night before as I lay in bed contemplating my tomorrow. This is another sensational time to do mental programming. Your conscious mind is most alert right before you call it a night.

In the process of consistently choosing to have awesome days, you will begin to see a shift in your thoughts, a shift in your behaviors and expectations, a shift in your life—an awesome shift! It becomes easier and easier! My college roommate and great friend Arvon Jordan puts it very clearly and very much into perspective. He always tells me that he made the move from average to awesome 20 years ago when he figured out that:

 …any day that he's blessed enough to wake up is an awesome, great day.

EXTRA AWESOME GIFT

I always affirm that the next day will be a great success. For instance, if I have a large class to facilitate, I affirm that the participants will be active learners, the information I provide will be useful to them, and I will do the best that I can. Throughout the day, I am consciously aware of my thoughts. Each time a worry pops into my head, I break it down to discover where it's coming from. Then I transform the worry into a more constructive and positive thought.

If I am facilitating the same material more than once in a day or a week, I make it less tedious by adding different activities for the participants. Negativity is virtually habitual in the corporate setting; therefore, I always include inspirational anecdotes and humor to lighten the mood of the classroom.

My motivation also comes from the photographs of smiling faces that are on my desk and cubicle walls. I have an extremely strong support system in my family and friends. Anytime I have a frustrating moment, I close my eyes and picture a loved one's smiling face, or I'll repeat to myself something happy that they said to me.

If I wake up in a sad mood, I bring a favorite CD with me to listen to in the car on my ride to work; I sing each song as loud as I can! In addition, whenever I feel restless, I direct my energy into creative endeavors: writing, singing and painting.

—*Assunta "Susie" F. Marino (Long Hill Township, NJ)*

Average: Waking up on the wrong side of the bed, jumping into the shower, jumping into the car and jumping into another day of what LIFE has waiting for you.

Awesome: Energetically beginning each day by reading something spiritual, inspirational, motivational or uplifting for 45–60 minutes; reviewing and creating new goals for yourself; going for a walk or working out. Buying a mirror and hanging it somewhere near the front door. Before leaving the house each day, looking at the mirror and saying to yourself, "I'm awesome and I'm going to have an awesome day! Awesome starts now!" Then confidently walking into your day expecting to have an awesome one and not letting anyone kidnap your joy and enthusiasm.

Quickly turn to your Personal Awesome Action Plan Page (p. 234) and write the five "awesome actions" you're going to take as a result of reading this chapter. When you're finished, turn back to read more about what it takes to go from average to awesome!

GIFT

Fire Hard, Kid!

You can't teach people to be winners if they want to be whiners.
Some things are innate. Simply do what you love and
you will be positive. It's almost impossible not to be.

—*Lisa Marzullo (Chicago, IL)*

"Come on Shooter, fire hard, kid," Mr. Sam used to bark as he encouraged his pitcher to strike out the opposing team's batter. "Come on son, fire hard!"

Mr. Sam's bellowing shouts of "fire hard, kid" could probably be heard for miles, all the way from West Philly to North Philly. This powerful phrase became the team's rallying cry whenever we wanted our pitcher to throw strikes. You could hear it from the players on the field. You could hear it from the guys on the bench. You could even hear it from the parents and fans in the stands. "Fire hard, kid." It became one word, said very quickly and loudly: *"firehardkid!"*

Mr. Sam's Jayhawks teams were an institution in West Philadelphia during the 1970s. You weren't considered a "real" ball player, we thought, until you wore a Jayhawks uniform. Hundreds of passersby would stop to watch our games.

Samuel Gallman was the Vince Lombardi, Billy Martin, Pat Summit and John Chaney of Little League baseball in West Philadelphia. The balding and graying, 40-something, six-foot-one husband and father was both a coach and an umpire. Mr. Sam, which is what everyone (adults and children) always called him, spent his summers teaching boys ages 10-18 about baseball, about life and about self-respect. And respect is what he deserved and received from us. No one, not the opposing coaches, not the neighborhood tough guys, tough girls and gang members, and certainly not the kids who played for or against him, ever disrespected the fiery coach.

But that didn't mean Mr. Sam's players were not targets for other abuse, fights and threats. We played in many games where the neighborhood bullies, both in uniform and in street clothes, reminded us during the game that if we won the game they would certainly win the fight afterward. Imagine innocent 12-year-olds at bat while the neighborhood thugs yelled through the fence, "You get a hit, Shorty, and I'm going to jack you up!" "Your mom is not going to be able to protect you. I'm going to kick your butt!" These were not just mind games. We often had to fight to get to our parents' cars and vans after the game. Mr. Sam was always in the thick of things, breaking up fights and doing his best to shield us from the hoodlums.

Nonetheless, with everything else Mr. Sam taught me, my most profound memory, the thing that still lingers in my mind, is the "fire hard, kid." One play typified this spirit. The score was tied with two outs in the last inning and I was on second base. My teammate got a clutch base hit. As the outfielder made the throw into home, I rounded third base. Stopping at third wasn't even an option because I was firing hard. But the play wasn't even close: I was going to be out by a mile. The catcher, all 6'2", 250 pounds-plus of him, caught the ball and waited for me to reach home plate. Sliding wasn't an option either, as I decided that the only way I was going to be safe would be to emerge the victor in a home plate collision with King Kong; I was 5'7", 140 pounds of energy and/or stupidity. I crashed into the mountain of a teenager with everything I had. I slithered down his massive body like ice cream sliding down a cone on a humid day. I hurt all over! The catcher never budged, but my slight, yet "fire hard" impact knocked the ball from his glove. I was safe! We won the game! I was, indeed, firing hard!

As I moved from my little league years through my teenage years to my adult years, I've always fired hard in whatever I did.

Merely showing up and only doing what I was asked was never enough. I always sat in the front of the class. I never believed in faking it until you make it. Pretending was for actors. We have to consistently and earnestly bring or give our absolute best, our "A game." And sometimes we have to weather the storm in the process. William Feather says that success seems to be largely a matter of hanging on after others have let go.

In my travels as a training consultant, I meet thousands of corporate, professional trainers. I usually share with them, early on, that I have good news and bad news. The good news is that there are thousands of good trainers out there. The bad news is that there are thousands of merely good trainers out there. I haven't come across nearly as many awesome trainers as I would have liked to, trainers who routinely "fire hard!"

Bob Pike, the highly respected and creative training techniques guru, once told me, after seeing me present, that I have more energy than any other trainer he's seen in his 40-plus years in the industry. This was after I had successfully auditioned for a spot on his coveted team of training professionals. My energy and drive comes from my mother saying, "There's always work to be done," and Mr. Sam yelling, "Fire hard, kid!"

I've done all sorts of things in the classroom and in front of audiences that suggest I'm firing hard. I've lowered the classroom lights and performed funerals for the participant's "doubts" and "time-wasters," burying those toxic items (which they've written on sheets of paper and have committed to purging from their minds) in shoeboxes, and then burning the remnants. From clapping hands, to stomping feet, to quickly changing seats, to the "sports clap," to the conga line, to the Soul Train review, to the triple kooshball review, participants *grow through* and not just *go through* my sessions.

I've gone from corporate to "cool" in front of participants' startled eyes when I discuss stereotyping and perceptions during diversity workshops. I change from wearing conservative Wall Street gear (i.e., conservative eye glasses, college ring, single-breasted gray suit, wing-tipped shoes, overly starched white shirt and power tie) to "yo baby yo baby yo" cool wear (i.e., dark sun glasses, earring, ripped t-shirt, pager, shorts, Malcolm X red, black and green hat and sneakers). I don't want to merely talk about stereotyping and perceptions, because that would not be firing hard or memorable; I want you to actually feel and see it.

During my keynote motivational talks I'm in perpetual motion, providing a real life visual aid for the points I drive home. I want participants to taste, feel, hear, smell and see the learning moments and directional tips. I want them to inhale the inspiration and inhale my energy! To that end, I lug cumbersome props and visuals with me around the world. People always ask me why I carry so much stuff. I just tell them that I'm firing hard. By the end of my sessions, participants are usually as exhausted as I am.

I often think about many of my colleagues who have secured mentors, attended professional development workshops, acquired various industry certifications, or taken lateral assignments to eventually move into the position they coveted. They were firing hard. I think of the many professionals I've met who have returned to school and to the workforce after rearing their children. They were firing hard, too.

When it comes to firing hard, Larry Boyd is a disciple. Much of that energy, Larry says, stems from his early childhood days in South Carolina. One particular school year, 1967-68, was crucial. The Civil Rights Movement and the Vietnam War were in full force. The public schools in Larry's tiny hometown and other southern states were also being integrated. From grades one through three Larry had attended all-black public schools. Just before he was about to start the fourth grade, his parents received the letter informing them that Larry would have to enroll in one of the integrated schools. Not wanting to leave his friends and start all over, Larry was initially extremely reluctant.

He was also fearful, because he had seen marching and rioting on television and firsthand.

Larry wanted no part of going to a white school. He said it wasn't that he did not want to be around white students. He just did not want to be someplace where he did not feel he was wanted. His parents even tried enrolling him in his old school on the first day of class but were told that all of his records had been sent to his new school. He had to attend school there.

His parents assured him that if he did his best everything would be all right. Larry started firing hard! He took this new opportunity as a challenge to show his new white classmates, his teacher and himself that he could excel academically and in any environment, despite the adversity. He was one of three black children in the class and he soared. He soared through his remaining years at the school and on through high school, college and the military. Larry, for the past 10-plus years, has been a manager for a successful international, non-profit organization in Philadelphia that coaches, develops, tutors and places talented minority college students in Fortune 25, 100 and 500 companies. He still maintains friendships with many of the students from his first integrated class. Several months ago, however, he took an extended leave of absence from the corporate world to return to the military to help his country in its war with Iraq.

There's an inner drive that moves us to move mountains. That drive moves us to study all night for a test after we haven't cracked the book for months. That drive moves us to spend all day cleaning up the house when we know guests are coming over that evening. That drive moved me to spend the Christmas and New Year's holidays hibernating in my office working on the revisions of this book when others were shopping, celebrating, vacationing or getting their "eggnog on." In essence, WE FIRE HARD WHEN WE WANT TO FIRE HARD.

As it relates to anything you do in life, if you want to create the possibility for awesome results you have to "fire hard, kid." If it means

Average: Settling for good results. Only "firing hard" during emergencies or when someone is watching.

Awesome: Giving your best effort regardless of the circumstances. Promising yourself, challenging yourself and reminding yourself to consistently fire hard, kid!

getting up super-early... if it means rewriting your class notes for the third time... if it means telling your friends that you will have to get together with them another time... if it means staying in on an absolutely gorgeous Saturday afternoon to finish studying or writing... if it means carrying additional props and supplies to make your presentations more memorable and outstanding... if it means doing tons of additional research before you interview for a job... and even if it means working for a boss or dealing with a professor or teacher who you *let* drive you batty, you still have to "fire hard, kid."

EXTRA AWESOME GIFT

What makes me go from ordinary to extraordinary is the EXTRA. The extra effort and energy to raise the bar, to go 110%, I believe comes from attitude. I find that quotes help me be in the top 2%. So I encourage others to find those words that inspire you and reflect on the message daily and soon you will be performing at 110%. Some of my favorite quotes are:

"If you can't see the bright side, polish the dull side!"

"Kind words make good echoes!"

"We stand tallest when we stoop to help others!"

"Setbacks pave the way for comebacks!"

—Doug McCallum (Lincoln, NE)

Quickly turn to your Personal Awesome Action Plan Page (p. 234) and write the five "awesome actions" you're going to take as a result of reading this chapter. When you're finished, turn back to read more about what it takes to go from average to awesome!

7 GIFT

Start Playing More Reader Rabbit!

I keep a pretty good attitude about life by balancing out my personal life and my career. I keep burnout at a distance by engaging in the numerous activities outside of work that I enjoy.

—Tina M. Greene (Binghamton, NY)

If I had kept a running count I would say that it happened nine out of ten times: whenever I was working in my home office, my six-year-old (at the time) daughter Daecia would ecstatically skip down the stairs and into the room and ask (as only a precious little daddy's girl could), "Daddy, can we play Reader Rabbit?" And nine times out of ten, I would say, "Baby, Daddy is busy right now, we can play later." We both knew, however, that my "laters" were synonymous with: "one day," "some day," "in five minutes," "eventually," and "when I get around to it." Dejected, she would slowly walk out, retreating upstairs to look for something else to do.

Over time, Daecia would come down to my office just to kiss me and tell me that she loves me. Her mini, non-Reader Rabbit-focused visits were obviously in response to my workaholic, insensitive regimen. One day, however, the gorgeous little kissing bandit came down to my office when I was in the midst of client calls, computer problems and chaos. Before she could kiss and run, I grabbed her and said, "'Let's play some Reader Rabbit." Her two-teeth-missing smile and boisterous "YES!" lit up the room like a light turned on in the bedroom in the middle of the night. She plopped down on my lap in front, commandeered the mouse and we had a Reader Rabbit great time. I had learned another valuable lesson.

We are awfully busy these days. We're too busy to take care of ourselves and we're too busy to make time for the people who mean the most to us. This era of rapidly advancing technology has eliminated the B word (balance) from our vocabulary. Some of us feel guilty if we're not working. Where is the balance?

We take power naps. We multi-task. We skip lunch. There are times when my flights land well after midnight. Arriving either at home or at a client site that late at night or that early in the morning is saddening. But arriving with hundreds of other workaholics is even more distressing. Sometimes I have to check my watch. The number of travelers in the airport would lead you to believe that it was mid-afternoon. The airports are packed with professionals too busy to enjoy life outside of their corporate responsibilities, black berries, palm pilots, laptops, pagers and cell phones. Sad, but true!

How are we going to savor our moments if we don't create them?

Daecia's desire to have more Reader Rabbit moments with her father was the slap in the face that I needed. I was practically living on the road; she helped me to realize that I was creating distance even when I was close—I behaved like I was still on the road when I was at home. My office became my sanctuary. With my desktop computer, fax machine, printer, television, stereo, telephones, a window, a bookshelf filled with resources, and a refrigerator close by, I was set. I would only come out to the world to eat, go to the bathroom and sleep. It was not uncommon for me to finally close down my office at 2:00 AM.

I had become a product of my insane society—always on the run, always in an airport, always rushing through conversations, always on the cell phone, always going to another meeting, always getting my morning workout in before 6:00 AM, always wolfing down my food and always awakening before my wake-up call. I convinced myself that this was short-term pain for long-term gain. But who was I fooling? I had forgotten what my former manager, Kathy Cook, had told me—to work smarter, not always harder.

You receive myriad lessons in your lifetime, and many of the most powerful lessons originate from the little hearts and minds of people who are too young to drink, drive or stay up past 8:00 PM. These little people love you in spite of your moments of anger, forgetfulness, morning breath, insensitivity and poor time management.

Workaholics (a.k.a. work-and-family-balance dodgers)—you know who you are–repeat after me:

- I'm going to start making more time for the people I love.
- I'm going to start making more time for me.
- I'm going to slow down.
- I'm not going to make a "to-do" list every day.
- Sometimes, I'm going to wake up and just do nothing.
- I'm going to listen to more music and listen to the birds chirping.
- I'm going to read more positive, uplifting books.
- I'm going to go for more morning walks.
- I'm going to stop getting wake-up calls every day.
- I'm going to stop checking my stocks every day.
- I'm going to stop getting upset if I don't get a chance to check my e-mails every day.
- I'm going to stop gobbling down my meals.
- I'm going to start giving my undivided attention to the person I'm speaking to.
- I'm going to start playing more Reader Rabbit!

Life is gone too soon. Your life meter is always running.

The quality times you spend with your loved ones are the coins that are needed to help keep your life meter running.

You're not going to believe this, but while I was writing this chapter Daecia came into my office to play. What perfect timing! I did take a break, played some Reader Rabbit, savored the moment we just shared and returned to writing *From Average to Awesome,* but not right away. We had dinner first.

How could I have been so negligent for so long? Daecia is my only child. I wasn't blessed with her life until I was in my 30s. I had desperately wanted a child, and this was my way of showing my appreciation? Moreover, the relationship a little girl has with her dad is precious and confirming.

Daecia still visits me in my office every morning that she can after she dresses for school to show me what she's wearing and get my approval. Upon arriving home from school she makes a beeline back to my office to do her kissing bandit thing. And a couple of her other favorite pastimes include rubbing my bald-head, at any given moment, and giving me Noxzema facials.

My dad was not always there for me, so you would think I might have learned from that sobering reality. Shortly after our Reader Rabbit life-lesson I drove Daecia to school. I make it a habit to either drop her off or pick her up when I'm not collecting frequent flier miles, flying to another client site. While we were riding, she totally caught me off guard by saying, "Daddy, tell me a story about what you learned from Grammy." I almost brought the car to a complete stop, floored by her poignant, thoughtful question. After I answered, fighting back one of the biggest smiles I've had since she was born, I winked at her through the rear view mirror.

As if she was on a roll, and I was a guest on her talk show, she fired Question #2 saying, "Daddy, tell me about what you and Uncle Rah Rah (my brother Rodney) used to do when you were small—what toys did you play with?" My G. I. Joe, Rock 'Em Sock 'Em Robots and Hot Wheels answer cracked her up and was the sensational start to the day we both needed.

We can't get the time back. Turn in your 24/7-work-membership card. If more of us ripped those cards to shreds, we could eliminate such sardonic refrains as: "I owe, I owe, it's off to work I go" or, "I work, I work, I'm becoming an insensitive jerk." Regain your balance. Create a place for rest and replenishment. You cannot be awesome if you're consistently working around the clock.

Thanks for the reminder, Daecia!

Average: Fitting everyone in around your schedule.

Awesome: Consistently making quality time for yourself and for the people you love. Identifying the things you do that take precious time away from you and your special people. Developing and following through with a plan for removing those things from your schedule.

EXTRA AWESOME GIFT

My attitude really went to a different level in May of 1999 when my son, John Willis II, was born. He lived for 30 days, but influenced more people in his 30 days than I have in my lifetime. He showed me that I have the chance to use his life as a way to influence people in my life. My desire is to influence children in this world as much as I can. I have a picture on my desk from SUCCESSORIES that says, "Priorities—A hundred years from now it will not matter what my bank account was, the sort of house I lived in, or the kind of car I drove…but the world may be different because I was important in the life of a child."

I have two children, Lauren (6) and Matthew (4) and my influence on them and any other child I encounter is what drives me to create a positive and outstanding environment around me.

—Jey Willis (Atlanta, GA)

Quickly turn to your Personal Awesome Action Plan Page (p. 234) and write the five "awesome actions" you're going to take as a result of reading this chapter. When you're finished, turn back to read more about what it takes to go from average to awesome!

AWESOME REFLECTIONS PAGE...

8
GIFT

Stop Depositing Bad Checks

Set boundaries and live by them, but know when to be flexible and
when to stand firm. Also, don't put yourself on a pedestal.
Let someone else do that—it's safer that way.

—Laura Hughes (Lewiston, ID)

Have you ever bounced a check? No, not one where you made an
honest checkbook mistake, inadvertently thinking you had enough
money in your account to cover things. I'm referring to one of those
occasions when you knew your account was on "E" but you neverthe-
less, boldly, aimlessly wrote the check anyway. Your hope and prayer
was that miraculously, some way, somehow, you would be able to beg,
borrow or find the money to make the deposit into your account be-
fore the bank processed your rubbery piece of paper.

That's essentially what we do when we take on bad business. We
knowingly exercise poor judgment, associating with individuals or
taking on opportunities we know are not good for us, perhaps partici-
pating in something we know is going nowhere. Plain and simple—
we know we shouldn't go there! It's tantamount to interviewing for a
job with a company that has a huge "going out of business" sign in
the front window.

A few years ago, while I still worked full-time in the corporate world,
I occasionally took a personal day off from work to do a consulting,

training or speaking job. These jobs provided valuable entrepreneurial experience. Not only did these experiences give me a glimpse into what owning my own business would be like, they also served up opportunities to work with companies that viewed me as the hired gun, the outside consultant.

I stumbled onto one client, in particular, whom other consultants in the industry–as well as other employees in the client's company–insisted I should avoid.

People consistently told me that there was one department in the company that was "bad business." My colleagues said that taking on work for this company was okay, but taking on work for one particular senior leader was akin to bullfighting with a Kleenex, blindfolded. They said that this powerful, demanding, and extremely crass senior leader ran an extremely tight, autocratic ship. The word on the street was that the department was "Stepfordish."

This news caused me to hesitate for a day, reevaluating my former manager's warning about taking on bad business, but I moved forward anyway. Besides, the person who called with the opportunity was following up on a family member's referral. Her relative saw me facilitate a similar presentation when she and I both worked for the same firm. I decided to make my decision after the caller and I discussed the opportunity over lunch.

During lunch she said that her relative had blurted out over the phone, "…you have to get him…he's outstanding!" Moreover, my future client was an extremely warm and caring person. She created an awesome vision for me for future work with the company. I was salivating over the prospect of repeat business, especially since I was exploring starting my own business. My first extended client opportunity!

We connected immediately. I was going in!

I presented a seamless case to myself. My closing argument was phenomenal. I convinced myself that my style was different from the consultants who had gone into this snake pit before me. My style was more energizing, more participant-driven, I reasoned. Based on the many successes I'd had with my full-time employers, I believed that I was ready for a challenging client—a stretch assignment. This would be another opportunity to test my skill set and would certainly help once I finally went out on my own.

The contract was for two engagements: one was a lunchtime train-the-trainer session for their corporate trainers; the other, a motivational keynote for the entire "risky business" department. I saw opportunity, not suicide. I envisioned high fives, not finger-pointing. This was a chance to put a major Fortune 100 company at the top of my referral list, not at the back of my mind.

As I'd hoped, the first session rocked! Kudos, smiles, plaudits and handshakes were plentiful. I felt relieved and sensational. I did it! Conversations and plans for my returning on a monthly basis were immediately underway. What were my colleagues talking about, I thought? It was just a matter of truly believing in oneself.

Round two was different. Ding! Ding!

I facilitated the 60-minute keynote, motivational presentation for the "risky business" department. Non-stop, I energetically and passionately shared encouraging words of hope, action and direction. I got the participants involved, inspired, clapping their hands and laughing. After the final, "Thank you," they gave me a standing ovation. I did it…I did it…I did it again, I thought. I was glad I took the risk. Many motivational sayings were dancing in my mind. "Obstacles are what you see when you take your eyes off of your goals." "No one can make you feel inferior without your consent." "Only those who risk going too far will ever know how far they can go." My colleagues were mistaken again.

One of the other client managers even walked me around the room, introducing me to several of the managers who had lingered around the lunch spread. I was taking my Cal Ripken victory lap and feeling the thrill of victory.

Little did I know how soon my exultation would be squelched by the agony of defeat.

I asked one of the pretzel-munching managers what he thought about the presentation. He hesitated, then said, "Jim, I thought it was great. Quite frankly though, it doesn't make any difference what I or anyone else thinks, it's what Hal Stern (the senior leader) thinks that matters."

I was stunned, wondering if the standing ovation I had received minutes earlier was live or Memorex. He continued, "Look outside, it's sunny right? If Mr. Stern said that it was snowing right now everyone else in the department would rush to leave the office immediately to avoid the traffic jams caused by the inclement weather. Sounds strange doesn't it? But that's the way things are around here." He said to wait a few days. The verdict would soon be in.

Upon my return to my office later that afternoon, I was welcomed by a voice mail message from the client manager whom I had taken to lunch. She was calling to talk about the session. Bubbling with enthusiasm, she said that in her opinion, I was incredible! She said the session was just what they wanted and that I had really delivered. Whew, I was relieved!

The next day my check bounced.

When I called back to get additional feedback, my calls were not returned. I then received another call from the same client manager who had left the "vote of confidence" voice mail. She reminded me that I left some of my props in their conference room and that I should come in to pick them up. I immediately heard the change in her voice—from cheerleader to the foreman of the jury. "What was that about?" I asked myself.

The overdraft notice and the verdict had come in at the same time.

She said that Mr. Stern loathed the presentation. He had several peculiar, choice words that I believed were targeted at me both personally and professionally—words that I had heard before to describe assertive, confident, black men. He said that I was pompous, insensitive, arrogant and self-centered. "Am I missing something?" I thought. "What do these adjectives have to do with the presentation? Didn't I receive a standing ovation?"

He went on to say that I was disrespectful for not asking for his permission to use his name in one of my examples. Huh?!?!?! In using his name, I said something like, "If I was Mr. Stern, I would want all of my employees to come to work fired up every day, prepared to make an incredible contribution to the organization."

In addition, he said that if I had known more about the organization's "family" culture, I would not have used the word "ass" in another example. He WAS right with that one. He concluded his feedback with a clear, "stern" insistence that I never use his organization as a recommendation or referral. To say I was incensed would belabor the obvious. It's like saying Jamie Fox deserved the Oscar for *Ray*, that Celine Dion can sing, that Maya Angelou writes beautiful poetry, or that Jackie Chan does a lot of stunts. Duh!

To further complicate matters, my two other client managers (who were both black) refused to return my calls. Communicating strictly through the first manager (also black), they told her to inform me that my presentation had made things miserable for them in the office because they were responsible for my being there, and that I would probably be the last black consultant to do work there. You've got to be kidding, I thought. Did the hands of time just turn back 75 years?

Mr. Stern (who was white) had called them all into his office and questioned their judgment for bringing me in. He was going to reconsider their upcoming promotions and they would have to run future consultant choices by him. I eventually, briefly, spoke to one of the managers who had been avoiding my calls. He began our discussion in a scolding manner saying, "Didn't I tell you not to..."

This experience was beginning to smell awfully foul. The entire ordeal had "bad check" written all over it.

I was having a nightmare, but I had deposited the bad check. I let that incident rock my desire to continue motivational speaking. I had a 2,880-minute pity party. I temporarily forgot that someone's opinion of you does not have to become your reality. Nonetheless, within a couple of days, I really got mad, got sad, got better, then got busy.

I deeply pondered Mr. Stern's targeted feedback. Some of it, I had to admit, was accurate, but most of it felt personal. I thought about the two client managers who did a complete about-face, initially showering me with praise, then with silence. I wondered what their jobs would be like going forward and how it must be to work in that kind of "camouflaged" wholesome, yet clearly hostile, environment. Although I was livid over what had happened, in a way I felt sorry for them.

As their consultant, I was not going to pay that same price to assimilate. That would have been killing my soul, my spirit, my energy, me. I was not willing to give up my values, my beliefs and myself to become the type of speaker Mr. Stern would appreciate. That price was too high! But it was a price, I sensed, that they were paying every day. Alice Walker's poem resonated in my mind:

"No man is your friend who demands your silence,
or denies your right to grow."

Were my two presentations that vastly different? I also considered the frigid reception I received from the others in the department when I returned to retrieve my supplies. From hero to zero, champ to chump in less than a week. Most importantly, however, I thought about the colleagues who had warned me that this opportunity was bad business…not to deposit the bad check.

I called Kathy Cook and explained what happened. Rather than spending time telling me, "I told you so," she asked me what I had learned from this experience. My answer was extremely heartfelt. I told her that I couldn't help but think that race had played a role in what happened. The senior leader's feedback was too personal. If his feedback had been more pointed toward my behavior, my information, materials and ideas, and not my character, I would have felt differently. I just felt weird about the whole experience. My gut suggested that he was more than just a dissatisfied customer.

Kathy listened intently because she knew I seldom used race to substantiate my corporate misfortunes. People of color often feel race is the only reason for corporate crashes. Race *is* sometimes the reason, but it's not the only possible reason. People of color, at times, rush to the race case rather than rushing to exploration, making sincere efforts to uncover what else could be causing their dilemma. But, after exploring every conceivable option imaginable, I decided that race *was* my final answer. It was my story and I was sticking to it.

I told her that the entire experience made me feel sick. I believed Mr. Stern was holding me, for some reason, to a different standard. He had shut down the entire system. They gave me a standing ovation. In no corporate culture would they do that just to be polite.

I told her how astonished I was by the behavior of the other blacks who had worked with me on the project. They certainly were not going to jeopardize their jobs (why should it have to come to that?) for my sake.

I even owned my part of the mess. I could have said rear-end instead of "ass." But, I went from standing ovation to standing in the cold. It was like a punch-in-the-gut. I did not think my sentence was just.

Kathy said that one of the reasons I did so well with my other full-time employers was that my white colleagues had the opportunity to get to know me…to trust and respect me…to see me in action, time and time again. "By getting to know you they got a chance to get to know your character and find out what you were all about," she continued. "Owning your own business, especially one that involves speaking and consulting, sometimes means being flexible, altering your style when you have to, to suit the client's needs. But you have to be true to yourself. Still, Jim, it was bad business. Everyone told you not to go in there! Some lessons are painful, aren't they?" We laughed. But deep inside I was still reeling.

Let me share with you the "after-Kathy" quiet conversation I had with myself, because although this was a bad-check-depositing experience, it felt like a lot more:

"Is this stuff (i.e., prejudice) ever going to stop? I don't let everything get to me—I'm not super sensitive-but some things leave deep wounds. This was just plain stupid! Just when I'd thought I had built an internal force-field to repel ignorant, prejudicial treatment, I was done in again. All my other race-related experiences, I thought, were the dress rehearsals. I thought I had moved to a place where sticks and stones could break my bones but racial names and games could never hurt me. I've had 13 years of corporate experience and 36 years (at that point) of living. I was about to start my own business. And what about all of my years as a diversity consultant? Nothing has ever affected me as strongly as this episode. One powerful, 'stern,' man reminded me that life's not fair. But I'll get through it. I have to! There is a blessin' in every lesson."

Sometimes rose-colored glasses are difficult to remove. Nevertheless you've got to "see the forest for the trees," "wake up and smell the coffee," and "don't take on bad business." Knowingly exercising poor judgment comes back to bite you every time.

Resist those urges (you know what urges I'm talking about). Avoid thinking that your "fate credit card" will never max out. Know that some situations are totally out of your control. You don't always have to be a Braveheart or Wonder Woman. Start managing your life's checkbook better! Stop depositing bad checks!

Average: Jumping into the fray without doing your homework, relying solely on your instincts and talents.

Awesome: Using sound judgment. Considering the wisdom of people you believe in and not ignoring the obvious. Developing a keen sense for what's right and what's wrong. Remembering that sometimes no matter how promising an action may seem, it's not for you.

EXTRA AWESOME GIFT

Throughout my career I've had a number of opportunities to manage people and have found myself making some consistent mistakes. I have selected individuals without enough objectivity and rigor. Several years ago I was involved in filling a key position in my company and was under pressure to do it quickly. We were committed to finding a diverse pool of candidates although, because of the assignment and the war for talent, we knew it would be difficult. When an African-American female candidate was presented to us by the Search Firm, we were so thrilled that we didn't do the usual due diligence to ensure that this would be the right hire for us. We were too emotionally invested—and ended up with an individual who was a complete mismatch with our company culture, and with a lot of heartache on both sides of the process.

I have given under-performers too much rope and then personally taken up the slack. I consider myself a person who possesses a fair bit of emotional intelligence, with the ability to size up people well. Having said that, I have on more than one occasion given people the benefit of the doubt way beyond what was reasonable.

In one particular case, I hired a well-regarded consultant for a significant fee. He was extremely effective in his interactions with the senior management team but gave little attention to the details and follow-up work that were also part of our agreement. However, given his popularity within the company, I resisted confronting him until I realized that I was over-functioning and doing 50% of what I had hired him to do. Eventually I had to sever the relationship but I should have done it much sooner.

—Ann Perington (Orange, CA)

Quickly turn to your Personal Awesome Action Plan Page (p. 235) and write the five "awesome actions" you're going to take as a result of reading this chapter. When you're finished, turn back to read more about what it takes to go from average to awesome!

GIFT

Say Cheese!

It's simple: I love, love, love, love feeling good!
When I smile and laugh I come alive.
And when I'm alive everyone around me comes alive
and then I really feel good.

—Aileen Dizon (Sacramento, CA)

The next time you're walking in a train station or airport, standing on a street corner, waiting for a bus or sitting at a traffic light, peer around slowly, security-camera-style. Do some people-watching. Look at their facial expressions, non-verbal communications and body language. Take note of the number of people you see smiling and those who look somber. Count the smiles. Total the frowns. The number of depressed-looking people will amaze you. It's frightening.

Just by looking around for that very, very brief moment, you're going to notice that eerie trend. I'm not sure if it's because of the anxiety-filled times we live in or the fact that myriad people tend to see the glass as half empty, but many, if not most, of the people you're going to spot will appear to be in a funky mood, annoyed, frustrated, late for something, mad at the world or wearing tight shoes that rub their corns the wrong way. Look around, and you'll see a great deal of defeat, depression and despair.

Why are so many of us in such a morbid state? People make it easy for me to develop anecdotes, metaphors and other material for my motivational keynotes. All I have to do is keep my eyes open and pay attention to what's going on around me.

I read a health and wellness periodical last year in which an article suggested that, on average, children laugh approximately 400 times a day. Adults, on the other hand, laugh approximately 15 times a day. Of course children don't have the same mammoth worries that we do. Other than during meals, their plates are never full. Their cars never break down. They don't have bad backs. They don't have to pay taxes. They don't have bills. They're not in sorry relationships. They don't get laid off, merged or acquired. No one is providing them with a steady diet of deplorable customer service. These, however, are just excuses adults make for their unhappiness. Stop! I once read that a happy and successful person is someone who can build a firm foundation with the bricks that others throw at him/her.

Smiling and laughing is such a leveling tool. Smiles and laughter are healthy, spontaneous expressions of life. Smiles really put people at ease. And the more you smile the easier it becomes. I love to laugh. I just love feeling good—not taking this world or myself so seriously.

In my field of work there are plenty of opportunities for me to take myself too seriously. Presenters, consultants, speakers and trainers carry their egos with them along with their briefcases, driver's licenses, evaluation forms and speech notes. But since we are so exposed, presenting in front of audiences of all sizes, we leave ourselves open for mistakes. We're very vulnerable. During presentations we trip, drop things, lose track of our thoughts and don't always know when our opened button or low zipper is providing a view into a part of our world that audience members shouldn't be seeing. Smiling, laughing and not taking those mishaps too seriously get me through those times.

I remember when a colleague forgot to take off his microphone during a session break. After we dismissed the group to their pagers, palm pilots and cell phones, he hurried to the bathroom, unfortunately forgetting to turn off his microphone in his haste. Those who stayed in the classroom during the break were treated to special bathroom sound effects. We heard it all, including the flush. Upon his return to the room, we all enjoyed a hearty laugh.

I also remember when another co-trainer, Lydia, inadvertently lifted her dress in front of the class. One of the participants had said something that was pretty funny and Lydia bent over laughing. While bending over she lowered her leader's guide to her knees, touching the bottom of her dress. When she raised the guide to resume training, she inadvertently grabbed the bottom of her dress, bringing it up above her waist along with her leader's guide. Her slip saved her from an even more embarrassing moment. The other comical part about this was that Lydia did not immediately realize what she had done. She kept training. Once we finally let her in on our little secret she blushed, turning a shade very close to burgundy, and responded, "That's why my mother always told me to wear clean underwear." We all laughed.

I learned many years ago that smiling could also be the serum for other ills. My mom told me some time ago to get into the habit of smiling, especially for identification photos. I believed then that Mom's main objective was to help others perceive me favorably—to help them feel comfortable with me. I would later find out that she had other reasons.

Yes, it was yet another one of her savvy lessons—to teach me to protect myself (you get more bees with honey) by flashing my 32 pearly-white teeth and two deep dimples. In any identification photo I've ever taken, I have always had a big, someone's-tickling-my-feet, smile. I believe those photos have had a positive impact on people and have erased some stereotypical thinking.

I meet many people during my workshops and speaking sessions. I'm still amazed at the overwhelming level of seriousness I encounter at the beginning of these sessions. The typical facilitator begins the session by saying good morning. The participants' customary reply is barely audible. Having mastered the routine, the facilitator repeats herself by saying good morning again. The participants, realizing they'd sounded like fans watching a golfer attempt a match-clinching, eight-foot putt at the Masters, respond by saying good morning louder.

Sometimes I wonder if participants see me more as a proctor for an SAT exam than as a management development consultant and motivational speaker. I show up to build them up, not tear them down. My goal is always the same: to help them personally and professionally.

I understand that there is a certain level of personal and professional tension before any workshop or event. The typical participant enters the workshop thinking, "Will I ask a stupid question?" "Will I learn what's being taught?" "Will I connect with the people at my table?" "Is this going to be worth it?" Or, "Why did my manager make me come here?" "I hope they finish early!" "I wonder if they're serving lunch."

One of my initial goals is to make that tension vanish immediately. I want to break into whatever they are preoccupied by. Many times, before the session gets started, I roam the room introducing myself. Sometimes I ask participants to handshake, high-five or hug at least 10 people they haven't yet met. That really helps them break through their pre-session comas. And if it is a group where everyone knows each other, the instructions vary just slightly: to handshake, high five or hug at least 10 people not sitting near you. I think it's strategic and responsible to begin your sessions before you start your sessions. The participants get so fired up and excited that it makes it extremely easy for me to then open with a bang.

I wear a smile every day. Laughter is one of the greatest preventative medicines there is. Laughter helps you feel better. Laughter moves all of the muscles in your body. When you laugh you create a positive expectation toward life. You have better thoughts, which lead to better actions, better behaviors and better results. And it's contagious.

Here's a case in point. Ten weeks away from home for pharmaceutical sales basic training (which included 24 exams) stood between

Carolyn Moss and her hitting the field as a pharmaceutical sales representative. Kathleen, the instructor, was, according to Carolyn, the epitome of enthusiasm and dedication.

Although Kathleen was five months pregnant, she still worked the group until 1:00 AM, making sure everyone felt comfortable with the material and overall job expectations. "Jim, there had to be times when she was frustrated, annoyed and lacking motivation, but you would have never known it," Carolyn said. "Swollen ankles and all! I've never felt more welcomed than when I joined the company. When my day turns blue, I think of Kathleen. Now, as a trainer, I hope to bring to the new trainees the same joy that she brought to my group. Her smile never went away!"

Start laughing right now and I guarantee that the people around you will start laughing too. Go ahead, laugh. See, I told you.

I laugh in my sessions and I laugh in my car. I laugh all the time and it feels awesome. The people around me are definitely affected. Once you start laughing and smiling more, you will see what I'm talking about. People will start hanging around you because they will want some of what they think you have.

Average: Looking serious, occasionally mustering up a smile. Only laughing when you watch funny movies, television shows or comedians.

Take a cue from the toddlers of this world. Their anthem, with regard to Bobby McPherrin, is, "Don't worry, be happy!" It's all relative. In the book *The Prophet,* Kahlil Gibran says that "the same things that bring you sorrow bring you joy." Stop appearing so serious. Watch the children. Watch the laughter. Watch the fun. Watch out, it's contagious. Say cheese! It's easy and it works! It helps you to move to awesome!

Awesome: Not taking life so seriously. Enjoying the people and things around you. Smiling and laughing just because you can. Not letting every minuscule thing set you off. Taking more deep breaths or just starting to laugh when you feel you're about to explode with anger.

EXTRA AWESOME GIFT

What keeps me awesome is mostly, I think, my choice not to be "awe-ful." I am a child of the North and, although I have traveled and lived around the world, I have never forgotten the happy, spirited, positive views of my childhood.

I come from a place where the sun follows the pattern of rest and run. This creates a sustaining abundance of light to fuel the harvest and the soul and the darkness that creates a balance of rest and reflection. This helps to spawn new possibilities as the green and pink aurora borealis dances in waves across the night sky's black stage. I come from a place where, for thousands of years before me, people developed personal mastery of their skills and learned to appreciate the harshness without which the beauty could not exist, where personal responsibility for self and others are twined in the thread of survival.

I come from a place where each day is a new canvas to be painted and I am compelled to paint.

I come from a place that reminds me that every person I meet will bring a gift of the community thread. I look for that gift and I look for opportunities to affirm the gift each person brings.

I come from an awesome place and it compels me every day to look with awe and appreciation at the goodness in people, places, circumstance and creation. It is this childhood sense of awe that now has language, and it has been translated into three simple things: appreciation, affirmation and abundance. Alaska lives in me and that is what keeps me awesome and what keeps me smiling.

—Catherine Woods (Union, NJ)

Quickly turn to your Personal Awesome Action Plan Page (p. 235) and write the five "awesome actions" you're going to take as a result of reading this chapter. When you're finished, turn back to read more about what it takes to go from average to awesome!

GIFT 10

Wear Your Own Jersey

I live each day choosing to be who I am.
For my life, the real meaning and sense of fulfillment come NOT from
what I choose to do, but from whom I CHOOSE TO BE. I don't let
other things or other people define me. I look for ways to connect with
people in a way that alters the air around us.

—Lisa Dommer (Columbus, OH)

I headed to David Kelliher's house to discuss my promotional video and website. My brother introduced me to Dave a couple of years ago, and we connected immediately. He has been my video and website manager ever since. Maybe it was the former jock thing (Dave played football for East Stroudsburg University), or the fact that we both have an amazing entrepreneurial spirit, having left our former employers to run our own businesses. We had already worked on several projects together, and we were meeting to strategize about the upcoming year.

I pulled into Dave's quiet, suburban driveway, unaware of the valuable life lesson I was going to take home with me along with all of my meeting notes. Life lessons are like relationships—they find you when you're not looking for them.

My 100% all-American friend, as he likes to refer to himself, is the epitome of thoroughness, organization and effective feedback. Dave met me at the door and we went straight upstairs to his office to work. After our long but extremely productive meeting, I packed my materials, walked down the steps and headed out the front door. As I walked toward my SUV, Dave caught me off-guard by asking, "What are you, a walking billboard for the NFL?" Startled, I said, "What are you talking about?" Before Dave could reply, I looked down at what I was wearing, and then realized what was up. I was wearing a replica Tampa Bay Buccaneers jersey with Warrick Dunn's name and number (28) and a Minnesota Vikings cap. All I needed was a pair of Philadelphia Eagles sweatpants and Dave would have been dead solid perfect.

But those were my walking clothes, my relaxing, "take it easy" gear. I dressed that morning thinking about comfort, not that I was going to look like an "ESPN Primetime" groupie. The thought that I resembled a page from a professional football team catalogue never crossed my mind when I took that last "vanity" look in the mirror before leaving the house.

Becoming defensive, I said, "Dave, I have a few jerseys that I sometimes wear and I collect hats wherever I go—this just happened to be the one I grabbed off of the shelf this morning." He laughed. "You're in denial Jim… do they pay you to do all of this marketing for them? And Warrick Dunn must be pretty special to you in order for you to want to walk around all day with his name on your back." That one stung!

"Dave is on to something," I thought. As if he were the professor and I were his student, I began to share my take-aways from his revelation. "You're right man, so many of us walk around wearing team jerseys with athletes' names on the back," I began, "and on the surface, you know, there doesn't appear to be anything wrong with that. But the sports stars don't know us… and probably couldn't care less. I wonder what would happen if we wore more clothes that said WHO WE ARE and WHAT WE ARE ABOUT."

"That's especially true for you, Jim," Dave said. "Since you have your own business, you should be wearing JIMPACT Enterprises stuff." Again, Dave's comment landed on GO.

I finished putting my meeting materials into my SUV, shook Dave's hand, put the key in the ignition and rolled the window down. "See you later, Warrick," Dave joked. "Dave, I got it, I got it," I replied with a laugh.

I had had another educational moment. I drove away with plenty on my mind and another chapter for the book and for my life. Thanks to Dave, I had yet another impromptu conversation with myself as I headed down the street, back home to New Jersey.

My "Jim talking to Jim" conversation sounded like this: "Jim, face it, you're a sports nut. Always have been. Sports have been a part of your life since you and Rodney used to turn your dining room into a basketball court. Remember the electric football marathons? How about playing touch football in the street? Drove your neighbors crazy, but that didn't stop you from diving on parked cars to catch the ball.

"You played half-ball, whiffle ball, dodge ball, baseball, basketball, football, step ball, wall ball—man you used to just play ball! Remember when you used to sit on the front step or lie in the bed listening to Phillies games on the radio, keeping the scorebook? Hey, what about when you were in college sitting through a boring lecture? You used to list the numbers 1–99 on a sheet of paper and write the name of an active sports star that wore that number. Number 44 was always Reggie Jackson. Number 6 was Dr. J. Now you collect team hats and you also have several team replica jerseys that you like wearing. Your favorites are your Houston Oilers Warren Moon jersey, your Wes Hopkins, Donovan McNabb and Jevon Kearse Philadelphia Eagles jersey, your Randy Moss Minnesota Vikings jersey, your Philadelphia Flyers Eric Lindros jersey and your New York Yankees shirt. You even have your own 1979–1982 Widener University and 1979 Philadelphia Daily News City football all-star game jerseys. Maybe Dave was playing with your head. Maybe you're blowing this thing way out of proportion."

But then another thought bungee-jumped into my head. It ended my inner turmoil.

During business trips I often get asked if I'm a fan of the team whose jersey or hat I'm wearing. My apparel has become a conversation starter. I never considered the significance of that before. Oh, wait…yes I did. During my senior year at Widener University, I used to wear prescription-less glasses, a blazer or preppy sweater and at times carry a briefcase. I wanted the faculty, administration and student body to see me as a student first and football player second.

So when business travelers ask me if that is my favorite team, I just say no… that I collect hats and this just happens to be the one I chose to wear. Sometimes I get into lengthy sports conversations because of the hat I'm wearing. Since I'm on the road so frequently, I meet tons of people in airports, in restaurants, on planes, and while waiting for taxis. What if they were asking about JIMPACT Enterprises, my interests and me rather than if I was a Philadelphia Flyers fan when I wore my number 88 Lindros jersey?

I'm not Tiger Woods. I don't want to be like Mike. I don't eat Chunky Soup because Donovan McNabb, his mother and the Eagles do. Yao Ming, Venus and Serena, Allen Iverson, Kevin Garnett, Derek Jeter, Andre Agassi, Terrell Owens and Peyton Manning are merely athletes that I root for. And don't be mistaken, I cheer as loudly as the most diehard fan. But that's it. When we wear their names on our backs, our admiration soars to another, frightening level. I can still hear Dave's words, "I never see them wearing your name on their backs."

You may be thinking that I'm exaggerating this point. But consider this: if we put as much time, focus and effort into developing and sharpening our skills as we do acquiring and wearing the latest team jersey, how much better would our professional realities be? Wearing your favorite team's jersey at the game is one thing—and wearing their hat and shirt during a championship run is another—but every day, every weekend, every night to bed? Come on!

It gets worse! Brand names, designer jeans, "Air-this" and "LeBron-that" and company logos are ubiquitous. Everything has a corporate logo slapped on it. You have the Staples Center, the Fleet Center, the

Wacovia Center, Heinz Field, Minute Maid Field, Citizen's Bank Park and Coors Field. What ever happened to the Boston Garden, the Astrodome, Mile High and Three Rivers Stadium? How long will it be before we say goodbye to Yankee Stadium, Wrigley Field, Fenway Park and Madison Square Garden? The Tweeter Center near Boston used to be called The Great Woods Center for the Performing Arts. I couldn't help but snicker when undisputed, middleweight boxing champion Bernard Hopkins had the name and telephone number of a gambling establishment painted on his back during a championship fight.

We're becoming all of the "stuff" that promotes superstars and the corporate world, yet drains our pockets and our focus. We work endless hours and save money for the privilege of promoting someone else. Consider the growing obsession with sports stars, entertainers and movie stars and the paraphernalia that goes along with it (t-shirts, throw-back jerseys, banners, posters, magazines and more). And when wearing their names on our backs or on our feet is not enough, we dress just like them. Some misguided people now get plastic surgery to look more like their favorite celebrities. Think of all the young girls dressing "babe-a-licious" to emulate Janet Jackson, J. Lo, Brittany Spears, Mary J'Blige, Pink and Christine Aguillera and all the young boys dressing like Jay-Z, Eminem, Nelly, Justin Timberlake, Usher and P. Diddy and other rap stars, all of whom present grossly distorted images of masculinity and femininity that kids aspire to. Quite an irony that in a country that claims to value the individual, we follow the fads with a mind-numbing conformity. We lose ourselves in the process. And if we're not dressing like them we're buying clothes from their clothing line.

Many of us could spend more time appreciating and loving ourselves—even marketing our own talents and abilities. Could doing something that appears so insignificant on the surface (i.e., limiting the team, designer and brand name apparel you routinely wear) begin to change what's in your head? I think so!

Average: Occasionally reading a self-development book or watching a movie, then vowing to make changes when you can fit them in to your schedule.

Awesome: Spending considerable amounts of time developing yourself and doing those things that stimulate others to want to connect with you for yourself, and not because of your team jersey or the designer outfits you wear. Situationally wearing team jerseys only to root your team on to victory.

Invest in yourself! Literally or figuratively invest in YOUR team. Buy a jersey with your name on it. Stay grounded. Stay centered. Wear a jersey that allows you to grow, to blossom and to realize your goals. Wear a jersey that creates opportunities for you to share your talents—one that draws people to you because of who you are and not because you root for a particular team. As the Indian sage Muktananda said, "Go everywhere, do everything, meet everyone, love everyone, but never forget to love yourself."

EXTRA AWESOME GIFT

People, my students, always knew what I was about. I've worn it on my sleeve forever. I still wear it today. I'm so predictable! I do things my way. Regardless of what's happening, I'm always on the positive side. I always walk away from negativity. I stay away from things that don't positively impact my thinking. People know I am who I am.

—*Dr. Frank "Tick" Coleman age 93, got his driver's license in 2001 at the age of 90; also had his left leg amputated that same year (Philadelphia, PA)*

Quickly turn to your Personal Awesome Action Plan Page (p. 235) and write the five "awesome actions" you're going to take as a result of reading this chapter. When you're finished, turn back to read more about what it takes to go from average to awesome!

11

GIFT

Say What You Mean and Mean What You Say

---

*After helping someone, I always look back to see who else is coming up
the hill. There's always someone else who could use your help.
I just like to be there, always encouraging and always giving directions.
And some of the feedback I'm going to give you is not always
going to be what you want to hear.*

—Dr. Frank "Tick" Coleman (Philadelphia, PA)

Can we talk? Be honest! Tell the truth! Level with me!

When people tell you that they are going to call you, and they
don't, are you surprised? You're probably more surprised when they
do call. Simply put, we live and work in a society where people don't
mean what they say and they don't say what they mean. What's more
disappointing is that you've come to accept and expect it.

How many times has someone promised you something and either
forgotten about it or come up short? We've all been disappointed by
unfilled promises such as: "I'll help you move." "Sure, you need help
staining your deck, I'm there." "I'll pick you up." "I'll be there in five
minutes." We're still waiting.

Next comes the tired, uninspiring, wishy-washy, pathetic, please
forgive me, excuse-laden, follow-up conversation that begins with the
inevitable, "I'm sorry." Stop making promises you know you're not
going to fulfill. I'd rather you tell me NO than create false expecta-

tions. Otherwise, expressions of intent followed by excuses become predictable and about as useful as an answering machine that has reached its full message capacity or an uncharged cell phone.

Just say what you mean and mean what you say. It's simple. If you say you're going to do something, DO IT.

We've grown too accustomed to people not coming through for us. People disappoint us more often than Simon tells *American Idol* hopefuls that they sound brutal. Listen closely and you'll be able to determine when it's about to happen again.

Take out your "try" detector. The word "try" gets used more often than a knife and fork at a steakhouse. "Try" has become the universal "get out of jail free" card. It's the most passive word in our language. The next time someone tells you that he or she is going to *try* to do something for you, run! No, seriously, start thinking about how you're going to do it by yourself. Would you want an accountant, on April 15th, to merely *try* to get your tax return ready for filing and mailing?

A friend recently told me that she never expects things from people– that way, she says, she's never disappointed. Wow, what a sobering way to live one's life! And of late, I've been co-signing that check. People just don't follow through or follow up. I'm not talking about building computers. I'm talking about building relationships.

My inexhaustible friend, Susie Fields, says that commitment and partnership are two of her major everyday practices. "When I take on something, I take it on!" she says. "Commitment is doing what you need to do even when you don't want to. I also create partnerships with people and I am an amazing support system to those in my network."

During my corporate days, I had managers who promised me promotions but reneged. One of my managers even held up the promotion letter for me to see, only to later say that I was mistaken, that I had misinterpreted what she was saying.

I once had a boss who, when I told her that I was considering post-ing to another job in our southeastern, Atlanta office, told me not to make a decision until she had the opportunity to speak to the senior vice president and get his thoughts. She said that she really wanted to keep me on her team and that I shouldn't do anything or say anything to the other office until she got back to me. About a week later, I eagerly walked into her office expecting to discover their plans for keeping me on board.

What happened next was as surprising as Mike Tyson biting off a chunk of Evander Holyfield's ear during their championship fight! My manager basically said *bon voyage*. She wished me well in my new assignment and said that the department really appreciated my contributions. She said the reason she had needed to speak to the senior vice president was to find out if they were going to replace me, and if so, would they do it internally or externally. I stood there motionless, like a child caught drawing pictures on the living room wall. I know I'm not a rocket scientist, but I'm not stupid! It was time for me to pack my bags. I couldn't get out of her office and out of that company fast enough. It was another corporate karate chop to the neck. I think that I was more angry than hurt this time. I turned down the other job because I wanted to finish grad school at home at Temple, but I resigned from the company four months later.

Professionally and personally, discard the following excuses. "Something unexpected came up." "I lost track of the time." "I couldn't leave… I didn't want to hurt his/her feelings." "I didn't know you needed it so soon." "You weren't clear enough." "I wasn't feeling that well."

Read some books on commitment, accountability and responsibility. Become focused! Become consistent! Become intentional! Become purposeful! Stop trying! Say what you mean and mean what you say. Your behavior will inspire others to do the same.

Average: Simply telling people that you are going to try to help them or support them in some task or endeavor, occasionally following through.

Awesome: Just doing it or telling people when you're not going to be able to do it. Understanding why you say "yes" when you want to say "no," and developing an action plan to change.

EXTRA AWESOME GIFT

*I value integrity. Above all, I always tell people to be true to themselves and to those around them. Honesty **IS** the best policy! Honor all of your commitments, not just some of them. **Never** break your word! Be straightforward in your dealings with others and you will improve the chances of being treated in kind. The universe provides the highest degree of support for and the strongest flow of positive energy to those individuals who value integrity and **live it** in their daily lives!*

—*Joe Sparacino (Philadelphia, PA)*

Quickly turn to your Personal Awesome Action Plan Page (p. 235) and write the five "awesome actions" you're going to take as a result of reading this chapter. When you're finished, turn back to read more about what it takes to go from average to awesome!

12

GIFT

Let Your Light Shine

Some people light up a room when they walk in and some people light up a room when they walk out.

—*author unknown*

There is so much work to do! There are so many people to serve! There are so many lives to assist! Let your light shine!

It's not a major undertaking. It doesn't even require a degree, tutoring, licensing or certification. We could do it daily simply by saying hello, opening a door, saying thank you, smiling, lending an ear or even by just showing up. The key is to place the focus on others.

My friend Amy Wilson has recently learned how to let her light shine through self-actualization. She discovered that she gets an enormous boost from helping others work through their personal issues and challenges. Amy says that knowing that her friends, coworkers and family truly depend on her and have come to trust her with their deepest feelings and thoughts makes her feel complete and valuable. She says it's a feeling that is stronger and more precious than money or material wealth.

I remember my after-work conversations with Edna, the 60-something grandmother who cleaned the offices of one of my former employers. She would tell me that I was one of the few people who spoke to her. She said that at times she felt invisible at the office. People would usually only speak to her when they wanted something—their desks wiped down, floors swept, etc. Edna and I would talk about her family, her weekend plans, just life in general. I didn't make time to speak to Edna to earn a humanitarian award or an interview with Oprah or Barbara Walters. I just did it because that's the way I was taught…to let my light shine.

Through discussions with Edna and Amy and others, I've come to know a number of unsung light shiners—and it's awesome watching them in action. My buddy Joe, the balding, always smiling, diehard Philadelphia Eagles fan and security guard, did his daily light shining as employees entered and left the building we worked in. He welcomed people with a smile, a hearty laugh, a score or a much-needed kind word. He often greeted people by opening the door and by lending a hand if their arms were full.

Hustling John, the sinewy, elderly, gregarious, teeth-missing, tattered-clothes-wearing, dependable paper guy, did his light shining on the corner of 8th & Vine every day as he sold the *Philadelphia Daily News* and shared laughs with motorists each morning. He always had a spirited thought to share and extra pep in his step. Seeing John each morning dodging cars and running through traffic lights, in any weather, to make sure motorists had their morning newspaper and motivational quote for the day, was often the propeller-starter for my day. These people would go out of their way for others. They were my friends, my people. Their occupations and stations in life were never going to preclude the blossoming of our friendships.

At one incredible stage in my life, my daily routine included seeing John in the morning when I bought my paper, Joe during the day and Edna right before I left the office to go home. They were great "pick-me-ups" whom I looked forward to seeing. They were such a positive force! I believe I connected with them more easily than did others in our corporate world because of my working-class background. From my life experiences, I knew that goodness, intelligence and integrity were not products of your salary but of your character.

Light shiners have a certain glow, a certain energy. It's contagious. Does that describe you?

"When my son Matt is sad in the morning or nervous about something coming up in school that day, I fill his hands with kisses," my friend Sandi said when I asked her how she shines her light on others. "I tell him that whenever he needs a kiss from me during the day he just needs to put his hand up to his cheek and he has a kiss to remind him how much he is loved. When my husband and I were dating, we decided that 11:11 would be our time. Whenever we were together and we saw that time we would tell each other how much we loved each other. If we weren't together and saw the time, we would send good thoughts to each other. Matt and I made a similar pact. 10:10 is our time. He knows that time is just shared between him and me and every time he sees 10:10 he comes running for 10 hugs and 10 kisses. Also, when my family is together in a crowd, and we want to say 'I love you' we tap or squeeze the person's hand three times and they, in return, tap or squeeze back three times."

"Giving of oneself is the most awesome, motivational force I can think of," Peggy Hazard once told me. I've known and worked with Peggy for the past seven years and the only time she's not helping someone is when she's sleeping. Her drive is unmatched! Professionally, she's a Managing Director of a major Philadelphia diversity-consulting firm. Personally, she's a Managing Director in building relationships doing volunteer and community work, partnering with not-for-profit organizations and letting her light shine, both domestically and internationally. She has traveled to places like Egypt, Ghana, South Africa, Brazil, Zimbabwe, China, Indonesia, Thailand and throughout Europe.

"We should take time to marvel at the transformation we can cause with a simple smile, a hug or a compliment," Peggy says. "I think of the beleaguered grocery clerk trainee who takes five minutes to find the price on not one but every produce item. Patrons' sighs and rolling eyes accumulate in the growing lines. You don't really feel like spending any additional time in line but you say, 'take your time, I know it's hard when you're first learning.' You can see his rigid muscles soften immediately… hear a sigh of relief… and watch a smile spread on his face as your light flows in. With just one sentence you have transformed him, not only in mind, but also in body. Then equally as awesome is the positive energy that enhances your own glow and spreads to the others in line. I know I'm exaggerating, but your bags even feel lighter. It's the little things that we can do each day that make the greatest difference."

In this era of corrupt business dealings and "look out for number one" attitudes this light-shining mission can often seem challenging for some. If that is your reality, here are seven super ways to let your light shine, professionally and personally:

- Always be prepared for a light-shining opportunity; it's better to be prepared and not have an opportunity than to have an opportunity and not be prepared.

 Listen to both the said and the unsaid.

- Do it before they ask you to.

- During conversations, make the person you're talking to feel like he/she is the most important person in your life at that moment.

- Empower yourself to reach back, reach over and reach up.

- Do not over-commit.

- Remember that people don't care how much you know until they know how much you care.

My buddy Alvin said that his vivacious fellow passenger, Mary, appeared to be on cloud 99 (even before the plane took off) as she took her seat across from him in first-class. Not a single passenger walked by her without receiving a smile or a wave. He overheard her telling one of the flight attendants that she had just put the bow on her birthday celebration with her family and that she was flying home to Charlotte. Mary asked for some champagne and nestled into her seat with the bubbly and the Sunday newspaper.

Later in the flight, Alvin said, he thought he heard someone sniffling, some crying, but wasn't quite sure. Then he heard it again. And again. He looked over and saw that Mary's eyes were wetter than a Seattle umbrella. Taking off his seatbelt, he went across to her seat and asked what was wrong. She was reading article upon article about the September 11th catastrophe and it was tearing her apart. "This is such a shame," she sobbed. "I can't believe all those people lost family members. It's just not fair." Alvin reached over, gave her a comforting hug, and told her that everything would be all right. He offered her the book he was reading, Mitch Albom's *tuesdays with Morrie*, and encouraged her to read it when she finished with the newspaper.

Alvin returned to his seat and Mary put down the newspaper and immediately dove into the book. When the plane landed, the two hugged again, Mary got off and Alvin continued on the flight to Philadelphia. A few weeks later a package from Charlotte arrived at Alvin's home. Mary had returned the book with a note that read, "Thank you very much for sharing this special book!" Alvin's light shone brightly.

Judi Hovde, one of my Minneapolis clients, and I were talking recently about what she likes most about her job. I met Judi at a training conference last year. She attended one of the sessions I facilitated on "How to Close with a BANG!" and we connected right away. Every time I saw her during the conference, she wore an infectious smile. As we talked she said, "Jim, in a workshop I once shared a very personal story… a story that I had not shared with anyone at work." Intrigued, I could not wait for her to continue. "As I was telling the story, I wondered to myself why I chose to talk about it, and why to this group at this time. The next day one of the attendees came to my desk and told me that because I had talked about my personal struggle with depression, she now felt capable of dealing with hers. That was awesome. This is the type of experience that keeps me going, knowing that in some small way I am making a difference in the lives of others. I just hope and pray for the continued opportunity to be awesome!"

My friend Jack Marinelli, who is also a corporate trainer, realizes the impact of his light-shining work. "Each time I facilitate, I remind myself that my information will undoubtedly help my participants with their patient care, their business relationships and the interactions they have with people in general," he once told me. "Sometimes

Average: Primarily focusing on oneself.

Awesome: Sharing yourself, your time, your wisdom and your energy with others as a way of life.

we see the fruit of our training immediately, while other times the benefits come farther down the road. Either way, it fuels my motivation to be even better in future sessions and to continually look for more creative and innovative ways to help my learners grow."

I know exactly what Judi and Jack are feeling. It's an exhilarating experience to help others in their development and to have them sprint up to you to express their sincere, heartfelt thanks after a session. I'm stunned, overwhelmed and somewhat embarrassed when this happens to me. I'm just letting my light shine and they give me way too much credit. They say that I've changed their lives and that I provided a much-needed boost. They also thank me for sharing so much of myself and for coming into their lives. I would not have it any other way.

EXTRA AWESOME GIFT

Loving your job has different meanings for various people. Helping people succeed has always been my motivating factor. My first job out of college was as a customer service representative, which, to me, is the most critical job in any organization. It's the first point of contact with the customer and the first chance to make an impact.

Since that time I have touched the lives of many, and every time that I see the end result, it motivates me to do more. I love George Bernard Shaw's quote, "I tell you that as long as I can conceive something better than myself I cannot be easy unless I am striving to bring it in to existence or clearing the way for it."

—*Hannah Gomberg (Bear, DE)*

Quickly turn to your Personal Awesome Action Plan Page (p.236) and write the five "awesome actions" you're going to take as a result of reading this chapter. When you're finished, turn back to read more about what it takes to go from average to awesome!

GIFT

Believe You Can Fly

---

*If anyone has the courage to take the risks and learn from the failures
necessary to discover their passions, talents, values and sense of destiny—
and will then bring their daily activities into alignment with those four
internal energy sources—they will have discovered a
foundational secret of self-motivation.*

—*Dave Arch (Lincoln, NE)*

The ballad "I Believe I Can Fly" is a masterpiece. The song crosses
cultural, gender, ethnic, racial and generational lines. It's a motiva-
tional speaker's anthem, lyric after lyric, verse after verse of personal
empowerment. The way this world is configured, if you're not making
it happen, you're either watching it happen or wondering what hap-
pened. To make it happen…you have to believe you can fly!

What prevents people from flapping their wings? Children believe
they can fly until they are socialized into a world of self– and soci-
ety–imposed limitations and doubt. Some children wake up in the
morning and go to bed at night to wing-clipping choruses of "you
can't do this and you can't do that." You cannot consistently perform
in a manner that is inconsistent with what you believe.

My mother gave me my wings a long time ago when she said,
"Jimmy, you can be whatever it is you want to be as long as you always
give your best and never give up."

I now believe I can fly because:

- I have faith in my God;
- I believe in me;
- I don't believe that we were put on this earth to fail;
- I'm a true romantic;
- I view life as one continuous journey;
- I know other people believe in me;
- I've cleared a number of life's challenging hurdles;
- I have an incredible support system;
- I know how to bounce back when I fly into negative vectors;
- I've seen what happens when you're disciplined and determined;
- I'm committed to being awesome.

My daughter, Daecia, is now getting her wings, too; I savor watching her flap and grow into them.

When I left my first employer after nine years to work for another prestigious firm, many of my colleagues thought I was insane. I had been promoted into management (the organization's minority management numbers were low at the time), was well thought of by people at all levels and was a mentor and role model for many people of color. Working in staff training and development afforded me the opportunity to travel to our offices across the country, so I had been able to establish an extremely large network. "Jim, you have it made, why would you leave?" they wondered out loud. "I Believe I Can Fly" had not been written at that point, but I believed I could fly on to other challenges.

My departure from my next employer was similar. I was working for a revered company performing extremely well in the financial arena. The organization was boiling over with creative, intelligent, dedicated professionals, and there were not many people of color in key leadership positions. I had an outstanding boss, a leadership position and a solid reputation. Confused and disillusioned, many of my colleagues confronted me with questions and comments: "Why are you going to leave us? Nobody leaves this company. We're a great firm. What about your partnership? Why leave this safe, suburban environment for what you will get in downtown Philadelphia?" Some considered my move to the city to be a significant step *down*, and they weren't shy in expressing that opinion. Nevertheless, I believed I could fly.

When, after 18 months, I left my vice president position in the city to begin a full-time consulting career with a black-owned diversity and management development firm, you guessed it—more of the same. People openly questioned why I would leave a secure job so quickly. I had been there a little less than two years. Why would I walk away from the huge corner office and a leadership position? Why? I had an entrepreneurial spirit and an intense desire to fly.

The company had been acquired and I had been offered a similar position with the new organization. But I wanted to soar, to flap my wings. My unwavering desire to move closer to running my own consulting and motivational speaking firm moved me to say goodbye to my vice president's title, my vice president's letterhead, my vice president's business cards and my classy vice president's corner office with the huge windows (ouch!).

Before I totally flew the coop and soared into running my own company, I experienced a series of suburban/city and corporate/consulting firm workplace differences that served as potholes along my journey to awesome. Nevertheless, I sensed that these speed bumps in the road would later lead to smoother travels.

I had not anticipated the tremendous difference between working in the suburbs, as I did for the first 12 years of my career, and working in the city. The corporate head games were the same, but the people were different (OK, here comes a ton of generalizations). My city colleagues were more "street-smart," more stern, walked faster and had a different edge to them. Their energy was different. Their conversations were different. The atmosphere was totally different! In the suburbs, I'd become used to seeing people sitting on benches, jogging or walking, and I had even observed wildlife during lunch. In the city I was now up close and personal with street vendors (selling Chinese food, fruit, CDs, pretzels, hotdogs, newspapers and more), shoppers, politicians, homeless people, police officers, protesters, activists and news reporters. I was surrounded by department stores and traffic instead of trees and hiking trails. With regard to the employee makeup, my new company had more diversity than my previous one, and their 10 years worth of diversity initiatives signaled to me that they were more serious about leveraging all of their talent. I adjusted to the change, but the differences were startling.

Initially, I found life to be vastly different working for my first black-owned firm. I certainly was not used to being in the majority. I felt like I could truly and totally be myself and finally take off the tight assimilation suit I'd worn for so long. For once, I actually had something in common with the CEO and managing partner, and it wasn't just gender and a love for sports.

I guess that because I was now in the majority, I felt a new, fresh sense of empowerment and support. I ceased calculating when to raise my hand or my voice during staff meetings. I did not feel as though I was always being judged. I did not feel management cared about the type of car I drove or the neighborhood I lived in. I felt that I could now talk to think, rather than having to always think before I talked. Moreover, I did not have that "walking-on-eggshells-keep-your-guard-up-at-all-times" corporate feeling I had grown accustomed to lugging around everyday.

After nearly two years of full-time diversity consulting with this organization, I believed I could fly again, this time, however, on my own. Everything I did for them I believed I could do on my own. I learned how to sell, how to manage client relationships and how to run a consulting practice, but I also learned that I wanted more *diversity* in my assignments. I remember my private conversations with Barry and Peggy (two members of the leadership team) about my desire to be a motivational speaker and author. I told them I wanted to travel around the world speaking and coaching. Shortly after those revealing conversations, I started JIMPACT Enterprises, LLC. They both said that they wanted to see me fly.

The black-owned consulting firm's second-guessers weren't as plentiful; the company was made up of a small collection of individual entrepreneurs and former corporate leaders. In addition, the company was considerably smaller than the larger corporations I had worked for previously. But I did believe that some of my former co-workers were waiting to be able to say, "I told you so."

They nearly got their wish. Y2K was a brutal year for me, professionally. I believe that the general economic downturn played a role. The numerous consulting and speaking opportunities I had lined up disappeared faster than the water in a marathoner's bottle after the race. Business and prospecting calls went unreturned. Proposals were declined and ignored, and I have to admit, second thoughts started flashing through my mind.

Pat and I were lying in bed watching a movie on some cable channel one night when the screen went blank, except for the message that reminded me that my cable payment was late. How embarrassing, I thought. But part of me got juiced over this bittersweet experience. I couldn't wait to use this anecdote in one of my sessions! I knew that eventually everything would turn around and I would be flying again. How could I pump up and challenge people to live their dreams, in spite of their perceived roadblocks, if I had not experienced any pain and hardships myself? How could I candidly tell people that fire is hot if I had not been burned myself? And that's been my routine. Endure the mishap, move on with even more vigor, then share the story with others to inspire them to GET BUSY!

Occasional subcontracting work with several consulting and training firms were my parachutes until my own business began to pick up. I did not have to play hide-and-go-seek with the creditors anymore. My bank was undoubtedly disappointed because my monthly bounced-check contributions were going to cease. And I was going to be able to keep a filled gas tank. I've always kidded with others that my barometer for being financially awesome is when the yellow/orange gas gauge light in my SUV (indicating that my gas tank was nearly empty) never comes on again. I believed I could fly.

Today JIMPACT Enterprises has taken off. We have our wings and the winds of commerce are moving in our favor. Speaking and consulting engagements are now a reality and not just wishful thinking. From Atlanta to Amsterdam, we have done work both domestically and internationally. I believe a large part is due to my belief that I can fly. I believe that whatever happens, as long as I believe in my God and myself, and have the support of my Titans, I will soar!

Previous successes help steady and strengthen our wings too, as well as the timing of our next flight. Unfortunately, many don't even consider flying to be a possibility. I read a business periodical a couple of years ago that suggested 85% of workers are in jobs they don't like. The study went on to say that 80% are in jobs where they only utilize 20% of their skill-sets each day. That's comparable to having a VCR and only knowing how to operate the power, play, and stop buttons. That's called under-employment.

Average: Settling for situations, either professional or personal, you're not happy with. Watching it happen.

Awesome: Surrounding yourself with other fliers. Reading books on empowerment and living one's dreams. Taking risks! Believing in yourself! Making it happen!

I believe professionals in the medical industry have determined that more heart attacks occur on Monday than on any other day of the week. Do you suppose that has anything to do with the number of people who dislike their jobs? How quickly do you think their weekends fly by? Can you imagine consistently working five days to live two? These are the folks who greet you on Monday mornings with a barely audible "hello," then follow that up with a vociferous, "I can't wait for the weekend to get here!"

Why do we settle for average? Why don't we believe we can fly? Why don't we believe we can touch the sky? I know we think about it every night and day…to spread our wings and fly away. We have to believe that we can soar to a better tomorrow.

EXTRA AWESOME GIFTS

I have seen the value of developing a willingness to take risks. Having fearful thoughts about doing something that is new or that has some personal risk associated with it is normal. But guess what? We can change our thoughts if we put our mind to work! As Susan Jeffers says in her book I Feel the Fear and Do It Anyway!, *"What I find more times than not is that the fear was not justified… it was just in my mind. The rewards for jumping out of my comfort zone were great!"*

—*Joe Sparacino (Philadelphia, PA)*

Growing up in West Texas, my dream of seeing the ocean seemed as remote as a college education, a fulfilling career, a nice home or a happy marriage. I always wondered if the waves really sounded like what you hear when you put a shell to your ear. I wondered if people actually lived the perfect lives that I saw on television. And I longed for a better life, just as I longed to feel the sand between my toes.

*Through my dreaming and believing and finally doing, I saw the ocean for the first time when I was 19. I stood on the shore with the sound of the sea echoing in my head and the grit of the beach on my feet. I was overwhelmed, excited and a little afraid. At that moment, I realized the world was full of endless possibilities if you BELIEVED. And just as I made my way to the beach, I **have** achieved many of the things I never thought possible.*

I often visit the beach now for reflection and more dreaming.

—*Trina Crockett (Austin, TX)*

Quickly turn to your Personal Awesome Action Plan Page (p. 236) and write the five "awesome actions" you're going to take as a result of reading this chapter. When you're finished, turn back to read more about what it takes to go from average to awesome!

14

GIFT

Some People are Just Not Going to Clap

I don't place too much emphasis on what others think of me; being respectful and kind to others, letting go of the past and the things I cannot change, are far more important.

—Tina M. Greene (Binghamton, NY)

I can easily recall many of the valuable lessons my mother and grandmothers poured into my head over the years. Unfortunately, my brain must have been on vacation when they warned me that not everyone was going to like me—and how their dislike could affect me, if I let it. I completely missed that one.

Like most teens who endured acne, high-water pants, awful plaid-and-stripe combinations, braces, jokes about weird-looking body parts, parent-contrived haircuts and fashion statements, I, too, dealt with verbal accosting by friends and classmates on a semi-regular basis. Call it kids being kids or kids having bought into the gross societal stereotypes and distortions about their race (i.e., internalized racism) or kids with way too much time on their hands, I can remember nonstop "busting" (i.e., making fun of each other) moments.

My three main tormentors in seventh and eighth grade were "Jelly Belly" Jesse Johnson, Walter "Let Go of My Eggo" Taylor and Anthony "The Slope" Carter. They, on a regular basis, used to call me "Lipton" because they said my bottom lip weighed a ton. And when that phrase about "loose lips sink ships" became popular, the James Smith lips bull's-eye got even wider. According to my friends, my lips could sink everything from the Titanic to the entire United States Navy. Somewhat frustrated at one point, I even asked my mom if I could get lip reduction surgery.

None of us understood at the time how deeply we had bought into mainstream standards of beauty and how this kind of teasing impacted our self-esteem.

With regard to courting, relationships, raging hormones and girls, I survived those too. I somehow managed to make it through my teen years even though I received my share of "No, thank you, I'm not interested" responses. But that was just a part of the growing-up, character-building process. My world then was not colored with poor self-esteem, negativity or doubt, just dogged determination.

That "doubt" needle moved back and forth a bit in college but fluctuated (E.K.G.-like) more dramatically when I entered corporate America in 1984. Initially as a marketing copywriter and then as a corporate trainer, I began an indefatigable mission to get my coworkers, colleagues and management members to like me and to respect me—in that order. Why? I would discover the answer later.

At first I thought I was merely being respectful, just doing the right thing, going out of my way to help people whenever and however I could. That's what I remembered my mother doing. If someone needed me, I would stay late and come in early, even when I didn't want to. Friendly? I gave more compliments than a smitten suitor. My "other-people-stuff to-do" list outnumbered the days *Gilligan* spent on the island. I did not realize that while I was accumulating a lot of friends, I was losing a lot of personal and professional power.

Things got worse!

When I first became a trainer, I would huddle up with the evaluations at the session's conclusion. If one person out of the 20 attendees scored the session low, I would be incredibly disappointed. It didn't matter if the other 19 thought that I walked on water. No, this did not have anything to do with me being a perfectionist; I wanted everyone to like me, to think that I was the most accomplished and friendliest corporate trainer on the planet. Moreover, it may have been a carry-over from my middle-school and college days, my yearning for acceptance in a world in which I was part of the minority.

I'd beat myself up over one disgruntled person. I'd make changes to the content and the facilitator's manual. I'd change my opener or alter my close. If the one or two people who'd scored the session only a "good" had left contact information on the evaluation form, I'd call them to arrange a meeting to discuss what I could have done differently. It didn't matter that my sessions continued to receive the most positive evaluations and accolades in my department; I was becoming an overreacting people-pleaser.

How did I finally change? Enter Jeanne Bray. Jeanne, my manager at the time, gave me one of those "developmental opportunity" projects. She challenged me to develop a workshop on assertiveness. That six-month journey changed my life forever. I learned a tremendous amount about my inner self and my inner drive. Through this journey I learned how I was perceived by others, about positive, powerful, influential language, and about how to teach people how to treat me.

I also used this deep research period of my life to get more involved with my organization's Minority Interchange Group (an affinity and leadership group for minority professionals) and to accumulate important information relating to my group identity and self-esteem in corporate America.

Through my digging I discovered numerous professional realities and challenges that are germane to everyone (e.g., dealing with stress, corporate politics, managing personal and professional responsibilities, managing issues of self-esteem and goal setting). I also uncovered professional pointers that, while helpful to the majority, could be much more challenging and laborious for African-Americans and other people of color in the workplace (e.g., pointers on corporate image, thinking style, appearance pitfalls, networking, managing one's personal life, obtaining informal mentors, acquiring information, marketing one's skills, survival tips).

Prior to my rebirth, many of my words and actions were non-committal, or what I thought people wanted to hear.

The keys to my evolution were these lessons in assertiveness:

 All CHANGES begin with a CHANGE in your self-concept; believe that you can CHANGE your outer reality of life by CHANGING your inner beliefs and attitudes

- People feed off of your confidence.

- You become the person you think, dream and write about.

 Your dominant thoughts will attract into your life the people and circumstances you need, when and in the form you need them

- Start making affirming statements like, "I think," "I believe," "I will," "I will not."

- Constantly feed your mind with the images, words, thoughts, information and aspirations you desire.

- There are distinct differences between assertiveness, aggression and passivity; part of being assertive is knowing when not to be.

I love collecting motivational quotes and I recently came across four quotes that, like an Andrea Bocelli aria, were music to my ears:

"All the water in the sea cannot sink a ship
unless the ship has a leak in it."

"The true self is always in motion like music, a river of life, changing,
moving, failing, suffering, learning, shining."

 "Many would rather be ruined by praise than saved by criticism."

"We cannot become what we need to be by remaining what we are."

I was evolving, but that did not mean that I wouldn't be tested again.

During my last corporate job I had to fire someone. Leigh worked as a training coordinator on my team. She was a warm and affable person, but when it came to consistent workplace performance, let's just say Leigh was closer to average than she was to awesome. After a number of critical mistakes, late arrivals, "dropped balls," extended lunches and marathon personal telephone calls, I spoke to Leigh at length regarding what needed to happen for her to keep her job. During that meeting and subsequent one-on-one meetings, she promised me she would quickly turn things around. Making matters worse for Leigh was the fact that my management peers were forming a "get rid of Leigh posse." Every time she made a mistake that had an impact on the department, their cries grew louder and louder.

I consulted with Human Resources. I consulted with some of my Titans. I talked with my boss, who kept saying that I had to consider the negative impact she was having on the entire department. Sometime during all of those conversations I realized why I was finding it so tremendously difficult to let her go: (1) my people-pleasing tendencies were resurfacing and (2) she was a black, single parent, raising a little boy on a modest salary. Some of the thoughts running through my mind included:

- We were in the holiday season. Could I hold off the firing squad until the New Year?

- My mother had successfully handled a number of single-parent challenges as she raised my brother and me. Could Leigh step up to this one?

- Why had no one addressed this situation before? Leigh joined the department before I did. Why was this situation left for the new guy, me, to handle it? Could Leigh's race have played a factor? Or did people think Leigh would say that her race was the reason people consistently questioned her performance?

After some deep thinking and another very serious one-on-one meeting, I gave Leigh one more chance. I emphatically explained to her how close she was to losing her job, that I had done all that I could conceivably do or would do. Two days later she took three hours for lunch to get her hair done. The next day, December 15th, I fired her. I thought about her little boy. I thought about her bills. I thought about the upcoming holidays. I thought about her future. But I also knew that I had to hold her accountable. Nevertheless, this entire episode still bothers me.

Occasionally, since then, I've had to manage other gut-checking moments during my journey. And although I have plenty of training and education under my belt, I have not yet graduated from life. As Ralph Waldo Emerson wrote, "The hero is the person who is immovably centered." That immovable center allows everything around it to move freely but provides an anchor.

My anchor is put to the test during many of the diversity sessions I lead. After one challenging diversity workshop that targeted race specifically, I wrote an article that was published in the *Next Step* diversity magazine, entitled "Malcolm, Martin and Tom: The Three Faces of a Black Male Diversity Consultant." What made the session so exasperating was that, after spending eight hours trying to support and protect the only white participants (three white females) in the room (there were six black participants), I was crushed when I read their session evaluations. To paraphrase their comments, they said I was confrontational, out of touch and there to start trouble.

The premise of my *Next Step* article was that it didn't make a difference what I said, what I wore, how much I smiled; certain people were going to view me as either Malcolm X, Dr. Martin Luther King, Jr. or Uncle Tom. Here is a sample of what I wrote:

"Over the years, I've had countless rewarding sessions with white audiences. We've laughed, cried and brainstormed many ways to leverage diversity in their organizations and in their personal lives. We've even, to an extent, explored race. The gold bracelet I wear on my left wrist during diversity sessions is a thank-you gift from a white male participant—his way of showing appreciation for my opening his eyes to aspects of diversity he had never considered before. But it's the painful, afflictive sessions that I unfortunately lose sleep over.

"Evaluations from those episodes cause me to wonder if I ever will be totally judged by the content of my character and my ability and not by the color of my skin. Some of my positive evaluations have drippings of stereotyping too. They say, 'He was great and non-threatening.' Who said I was going to be threatening? These are subliminal stereotypes trick-or-treating as positive evaluative remarks. If my agenda were to grind a race ax, then I would probably understand the emotional, pointed feedback better. Besides, confrontational, minority diversity consultants are as welcome as frustrated union protestors at a chess tournament.

"Some blacks have viewed me as a sell-out because they associate my words of optimism and encouragement with words of compromise and assimilation. They expect me to repetitiously validate the contention that they've been dogged by 'the white man,' and to publicly blame the institutional systems, structures and cultures they stomach everyday. When I don't present the facts as strongly as they'd like, I sense that they believe I'm all fluff and no stuff. If they feel I'm not pushing hard enough, they will take it upon themselves to turn up the volume. That's when I find myself playing lifeguard, monitoring the amount of time everyone (i.e., blacks, whites, Latinos, Asians, Hispanics, Native Americans) spends in the "race pool" conversation.

"...I find this journey to be incredibly challenging, exhausting, moving, yet rewarding. I wonder if I ever will be seen as someone other than Malcolm, Martin or Tom?"

Despite these challenges, I still have a job to do: to help ALL people move from average to awesome. I now travel nationally and internationally, meeting thousands of people, facilitating

Average: Being overly concerned with what people think of you and your ability. Over-reacting when someone doesn't like you or like what you've done.

Awesome: Developing an extremely strong, positive self-concept and affirming group identity. Staying centered and remembering that your beliefs become your reality. Knowing what your special sensitivities are and working hard to not let anyone get to you.

hundreds of workshops and doing motivational speaking. I'm in the zone. I'm the artist. Through my work, I passionately paint the picture and then stand back. Many people gasp with appreciation while others move on to the next painting (going back to their previous stressful life routines). Nevertheless, as long as I remain positive, centered and assertive, and believe I've done my best, I always win. I cannot be awesome if I'm always worrying about what other people think. Besides, some people are just not going to clap anyway. But that's OK.

EXTRA AWESOME GIFT

As a Human Resource manager who is consistently dealing with disgruntled employees who just don't believe they should have to work to receive a salary, I'm always dealing with drama. At times, I'm viewed as the bad cop. That's why I really put a lot of emphasis on those who truly appreciate their jobs. I have taken to writing thank-you notes to those associates just to remind them that they are doing a great job and to keep up the awesome work. The notes make a huge difference to the associates and their energy helps make it possible for me to deal positively with the employees who don't think I'm so awesome.

—*Adrianne Winter (San Ramon, CA)*

Quickly turn to your Personal Awesome Action Plan Page (p. 236) and write the five "awesome actions" you're going to take as a result of reading this chapter. When you're finished, turn back to read more about what it takes to go from average to awesome!

15
GIFT

Be Yourself, Because Everyone Else is Taken

*Be true to yourself, your values and your ideas. Strive to make a
difference no matter how small. Always be someone who adds value to
a situation or relationship—not someone who detracts from it. Always,
always maintain your integrity and dignity.*

—Sherry Nottingham (Philadelphia, PA)

I once asked my ex-wife to give me an example of when she felt as
though she wasn't being true to herself. Without hesitation, she said
when she felt pressure to be somebody she wasn't, just to make some-
one else happy. I continued my inquiry. "How did that make you
feel?" "I didn't like it…I felt phony and, depending how phony I was
being, I felt pretentious…just not good about myself," she said.

Over the years, I've met quite a few impostors, pretenders and
quick-change artists–people who are seldom themselves. Clearly there
are times when we all feel pressured to pretend to be someone we're
not. For whatever reason (fame, fear, survival, greed, love, low self-
esteem, collusion, corporate pressures) we can lose sight of the "to
thine own self be true" mantra. Below I describe the folks I've met
professionally. Have you met any of them?

Em U. Late:

These people want to be like Mike, striving to mirror the efforts,
style and/or mannerisms of their hero/heroine. They dress, walk, talk,

dance and yearn to perform and behave similarly. Being in the "say for pay" profession myself, I have a keen eye for speakers who shamelessly copy the routines, quips, quotes, gestures, delivery and movements of other speakers. And if they're not already thinking about cloning their idol, others push their "copy cat" snowball down the hill: "He's going to be the next (Letterman, Ali, Poitier)" or she's going to be the next (Nadia, Tyra, Aretha)" they offer. Nike, several years ago, even got the "I'm Tiger Woods" bandwagon rolling for a group of young impressionables.

Wyle Atwork:

Many admit they act differently while at work than they do at home. Over the years, Wyle has come to realize that what gets rewarded gets repeated—and then gets rewarded again. Wyle is a quick study, assessing and then performing similarly to those in his/her corporation. Since many of today's organizations are conservative, bottom-line, results oriented, Wyles usually work in corporate environments where these four factors tend to be at play:

- Work is primarily a goal-oriented activity.
- Power involves positions of authority and control of financial resources.
- Problem solving tends to focus on tasks and quick results, not necessarily on processes and people.
- Elitism, status and titles are used as a measure of valuing others.

Pretty soon Wyle's walk, talk, dress, work style, companions and interests change. The frustrated Wyles that I've met continually work to survive, evolve and fit in. This has a higher price when one's personal or cultural style is further from the corporate standard. Nearly every part of his/her every day is spent trying to perfect this corporate identity and shuffle. Wyles, over time, usually move from one organization to the next, until they soar, settle or start their own businesses. As a recovering Wyle, I learned that you can only pretend for so long. The costume eventually has to come off.

Pierre Pressure:

These people just want to fit in with their peer group and do whatever they must to fit in. They want to do "it" because that's what everyone else is doing. Changing their looks, their diet, their field of study, their exercise routine, their socializing habits and their interests are at the top of their lists. In order to fit in, they are prone to falsehoods and exaggeration. Eventually they grow tired of running on this uphill treadmill. They become remorseful, unfulfilled and depressed.

B. A. Jones:

This person lives to keep up with the other Joneses. It's mostly a materialistic mission. From automobiles to SUVs, from houses to decks, from desktop computers to laptop computers, from palm pilots to pagers, from VCRs to DVDs, from coats to clothes, from season tickets to timeshares, B. A. labors to duplicate and will go to ridiculous lengths to keep pace.

You'd better buy a security system for your accomplishments, as they are also fair game. B. A. Jones will attend the same schools, major in the same subjects, join the same organizations and associations, take up the same hobbies and even work out at the same sports clubs.

Hal Others-Seemee:

Hal, bless his heart, merely wants to put a smile on your face. Hal spends his life striving to live up to your expectations of him. Denying the interests, activities and pursuits that bring him joy, Hal will jump through fiery hoops to please you. On numerous occasions I've heard a Hal say he did something because someone else wanted him to. Somewhere along his journey, Hal forgot who he was. Hals change majors, change occupations, change partners and change their minds because you want them to. If you know a Hal, please share these two thoughts with him: "You were born an original; don't be a copy" (Rich Meiss) and, "When we are unable to find tranquillity within ourselves, it is useless to seek it elsewhere" (La Rochefoucauld).

Sherry Nottingham and I worked together at my last full-time job. My office was on one end of the floor and hers on the other end, but our outlook on life, passions and interests created a space for us to develop a beautiful friendship. We often talked about diversity (Sherry is Japanese-American), work and family balance and what it takes to be truly happy and fulfilled. During a recent conversation, Sherry, now a mother of three who left the corporate chaos to begin a family, says that being self-motivated drives her to be the person she is. "I have an inner drive; much of my motivation comes from within, so my competition is within myself to be the best that I possibly can be at all times and with all people with whom I come in contact.

Average: Living a life using other people's thoughts, perceptions and beliefs as your measuring stick.

Awesome: Developing your own identity and becoming the best possible YOU you can be. Buying a mirror and putting it somewhere near the front door—then looking at yourself in the mirror everyday before you head out into the world, to remind yourself that you're awesome and that you're going to be true to yourself.

"Having said that, I do my best to be true to myself, my values and my ideals. I live by the rule that we model the behavior that we would like to see others share in our presence (trust, honesty, integrity, etc.) as opposed to simply lecturing about the merits of such behavior. I strive for inner peace and nurture my spirit in part by knowing that every day when I look at myself in the mirror and when I go to sleep at night I can live with myself. Life presents many challenges with no right or wrong answers…where the lines are not clear and often are fuzzy and gray. Knowing, however, in my gut that I did the right thing as opposed to the popular thing is so much easier than struggling with the conflict of going against my heart and my gut."

You will not move from average to awesome if your life's quest is to pretend to be a person you're not. Love yourself. Take care of yourself. Be yourself, because everyone else is taken!

EXTRA AWESOME GIFT

While I am truly content with being me, I am even more a willful visionary. So to accept that who and where I am in life is all that was meant to be would be to deny my vision, which is something greater than the whole of me, and would only serve to keep me comfortably stuck. As I grow, I find it important to be gentle with myself and to appreciate where I began this life-long journey on the road to awesome.

One of the greatest motivators in reaching new heights is the intrinsic belief that I am worth it. The idea that I am a valuable, capable and lovable human being was personally a hard sell for many years, but by surrounding myself with people who were able to see and validate the beauty I possess, I eventually gained total buy-in, and was then able to radiate it beyond myself to benefit others.

Ultimately, what makes it all good and keeps me positive is all about perspective. I have the power to redefine any barrier or situation based on how I choose to perceive it and receive it.

—Kimberly Cortijo (Davis, CA)

Quickly turn to your Personal Awesome Action Plan Page (p. 236) and write the five "awesome actions" you're going to take as a result of reading this chapter. When you're finished, turn back to read more about what it takes to go from average to awesome!

16

GIFT

You're Not Always Going to Get the Best Hand

You can have horrible things happen to you, and I have.
But I have never let my past keep me down. I deal with it and I'm
completely resilient. I always hold my head up and
move forward faster and stronger.

—*Nancy Rebecca (Chicago, IL)*

Raise your right hand, right at this moment, if you've ever worked for a miserable manager. Stand up, right now, if you've ever worked in a lousy company. If you've ever felt that life was not fair, say to yourself, "Been there, done that; I've got the t-shirt and the hat."

Obviously, we're not always dealt the best hand or provided the best possible circumstances. What's significant, and I'm sure this will not be the first time you've heard this, is it's how you play your hand that counts.

Former Philadelphia high school coach and physical education teacher Steve Kane's playing cards were "The Bottom." That's what we called the West Philadelphia neighborhood where my high school, University City, was located. The students that attended the school were a combination of the gifted and the gritty. We had bookworms and bookies, scholars and schemers, the tough and the talented.

Kane coached the boys' tennis and girls' volleyball teams. For 27 years he was also the boy's basketball coach. The father of three and grandfather of five also became the adopted white father of nearly every black ballplayer who ever donned the Jaguars black and gold basketball uniform. During his years with the school, Steve's reality was the kind of black, urban drama captured in Spike Lee and John Singleton movies. Every year Kane tangled with gang violence, single-parent families, drugs, poverty, robberies, homelessness and low SAT scores.

Along with the obligatory college recruiting visits, the on and off court coaching, mentoring and tutoring, Coach Kane's unofficial job description included: delivering eulogies, providing bail money and rides home, buying clothes for his players, visiting wounded players' bedsides, interrupting drug deals and providing meals. His responsibilities extended beyond high school as he mentored many of his players while they pursued college degrees. He was in the stands at many of my college football games, coached me through the rigors of attending a predominantly white university and convinced me to buy my first pair of Docksiders. He also found time to win 347 games, coach numerous playoff teams and win the high school Public League Basketball Championship in 1995.

Upon joining the University City faculty in 1972, Steve found a predominantly black, inner-city school with lower-to lower-middle-class students, a lack of facilities and school tradition, and recurring gang violence. Considering the situation, he could have lobbied for an assignment in a more white, affluent, suburban environment. Time after time when his players' predicaments took precedence over his own personal life challenges, Steve could have packed his gym bag, put on his coat and hat and left. No one would have blamed him if he had transferred to a more prominent school, one that at least had its own football field. I remember those days where all of us–the varsity and junior varsity football teams, girls' field hockey teams and boys' soccer teams—practiced simultaneously on the same 50-yard long dirt hill called a field. However, until he retired in 1999, Steve played the hand he was dealt. And he played it extremely well. My teammates and other alumni loved him for it. He was even adopted by the residents of the "The Bottom" as their coach.

My brother once had a peculiar hand to play, too. He had graduated from the University of Pittsburgh in 1987 with a degree in Psychology and sought to obtain an MBA, with a focus on International Business. There were five immediate concerns, however. One, money. Two, money. Three and four, money. Five, there weren't many schools that offered the special, accelerated curriculum Rodney desired. He handled the fifth concern by choosing the University of Hartford.

Next, he had to wrestle, flip, take down and pin the other four. Oh, I left out one additional factor. Hartford informed him that part of his MBA course-work involved completing the first year's curriculum in Paris. I remember my mother looking at my brother's playing cards and cringing because of what she saw.

This was his hand: (1) in order to pay for the year in France he had to send his student loan money overseas and have it exchanged for French currency; (2) until that money arrived he would only have enough money to fly to Paris and live for a couple of days; (3) even with the student loan he would not have enough money to return home; (4) the only French he knew was "voulez-vous coucher avec moi ce soir?" (thanks Patti LaBelle); (5) he hadn't secured a place to stay, and without the money from the loan he couldn't afford to pay rent; and (6) he was the only African-American in his international business class of 50.

My mother, who is as cautious and risk-averse as they come, did not appreciate my cheering, "Go Rod Go! Go Rod Go!" from the sidelines.

Rodney looked at his hand one more time, then started playing. As soon as he arrived in France, he met an American who had an apartment for rent. The guy, coincidentally, was from the same Philadelphia neighborhood we had moved to when we left my dad. Hearing the financial dilemma Rodney was in, the man let him live rent-free for awhile. The "while" turned into "some time."

This was fantastic, but then his cards got worse.

After two months of non-payment, the school informed Rodney that if he were to continue in the program they would have to receive his tuition soon. That "soon" became two weeks. In the midst of this, however, his cards finally began to improve. Rod's survival instincts and amiable personality enabled him to connect and build relationships with his classmates. Those relationships grew to the point where Rodney was never in a situation where he had to worry about a meal, a study partner or a glass of wine. He also learned enough French to get by.

Rodney's student loan money arrived at last. The school got its tuition. The supportive landlord got his rent and in 18 months my brother got his MBA in International Business from the University of Hartford. Yes, he played his cards just right but it wasn't easy.

"Major frustration," Rodney said as he recounted the entire experience to me. "I wish that a non-sports related analogy came to mind but it doesn't so here it is. There were a number of obstacles, but to put it simply, I was a road team playing without its best players. The road was Paris, I was the team and my best players were my resources, my family, my friends, my language, my familiar housing and living conditions. And in the beginning I thought that I was going to win by attending Drexel University (in Philadelphia). Everything would have been familiar to me. Shortly after I began the Hartford MBA Program (because of the international experience and the accelerated degree program), I began to view the France experience much differently. I played to survive. I felt that if I had my resources, I would have been able to perform much, much better. I wasn't used to playing to keep the score close. I wasn't used to not going for the A. I found myself going for not failing, taking the sure shots. I decided to keep the score close until we played the second half on my home court in the States. I kept telling myself to hold on. I couldn't get knocked out. I had to hang on for six to nine months until I got home and got my best players back."

The Russell H. Conwell Middle Magnet (my junior high school) Crew met again during the Christmas holidays a couple of years ago. Every year this group of 1970's Survivors (usually somewhere between eight and ten of us attend) meet for dinner on the last Saturday of the year to check in, catch up and reminisce. I don't attend the event every year but when I do, it doesn't take too many minutes before I'm all caught up with everything about everybody.

Our playing cards included being a handful of black students attending a predominantly white middle school from 1973-1975. The hand appeared sensational on the outside (i.e., attending one of the academically best-rated middle schools in the city), but that's why playing cards have numbers on one side and generic colors on the back. The school was also located in one of the most racially divided, blue-collar areas of Philadelphia. My classmates were my first true affinity group. We protected, coached, tutored and loved each other…and we survived.

As I sat at the Warmdaddy's restaurant dinner table, I became mesmerized in the moment. The place was packed, the jazz was kicking, and the energy was electric. I looked around the table at Larry Horne and at Jessica Battle, at Tony Spann and at Charles Carr, at Deidre Graham and at Vanessa Faire, at Harry Kirby and at David Thomas. Recalling the stories about how we survived the neighborhood thugs, I moved from boisterous laughter to quiet tears.

Life wasn't hilarious or amusing back then. Nearly every day or every other day, we (like many of the Conwell students of color) were assaulted, roughed up or just barely escaped a severe beating from the white neighborhood toughs. They were the Fight Club and we were their fodder.

Most of us commuted to school on public transportation. Groups of grade-schoolers (girls and boys, mostly black but also Latino and Asian) walked slowly with schoolbooks in hand through the blue-collar white neighborhood, heading to the train, anticipating at any moment having to run or fight to get to safety. The ten-minute walk from the train to the school seemed like hours.

There was one additional depressing element to this ritual. Whenever the neighborhood white guys beat us up, several of the tough guys in our crew beat up the white, neighborhood Catholic school students who were still on the train when we boarded. Those students, their faces signaling trepidation and panic when we boarded the train frustrated and beaten, had to endure five long-drawn-out minutes of accosting and revenge before they reached their stop.

Conwell's annex (used for graphic arts, shop and home economics) was located two and a half blocks from the main building. Walking back and forth between buildings was our version of Russian roulette. When we traveled in a group alongside our white classmates, the neighborhood bullies and dropouts settled for staring at us and mouthing obscenities. When we traveled alone we were moving targets. If we were running late for class, let's just say we missed class that day. It was safer that way. Talk about having an awful playing hand. We were 12-13-and 14-year-old students. They were 17-18-19-and 20-year-old thugs.

My ex-wife, who had joined us for dinner, asked why we didn't just transfer to another school. As Larry explained, we all listened, nodding in agreement. "Pat, we formed a collective bond, a tight group," he said. "We were getting a great education and we WERE going to make it together."

I sat there, counting my blessings. I've never undervalued the significance of my mentally and physically escaping that racial war zone called a neighborhood. Nevertheless, I had heard these stories before. I had been on the receiving end of a lot of the many punches, kicks, rocks, snowballs, baseball bats, brass knuckles, taunts and threats. But since I was in the midst of writing this book, I was more reflective, sentimental and moved. I was proud of my classmates. We all graduated. We all survived. We all played the hand that was in front of us.

When I attended Widener University, I had to play another complicated hand. My cards included a predominantly white university, faculty and students. Regardless of how many friendships I developed, there were still many times when I felt lonely, with few people to talk to and few people who would understand or want to understand what it felt like to consistently be in the minority. I have many memories from those four years. My highlights: graduating on time with a degree in English; meeting a phenomenal English professor and mentor, Larry Kelly, who took over where Mrs. Brodie left off; winning a Division III National Championship in football and developing several incredible friendships. My low-lights were many of my card-playing experiences. I recall the time I was returning to my campus apartment after an evening of backgammon with some friends. There was a party going on next door. The door was open and the music was blasting. I took a quick peak inside and made eye contact with one of the gregarious party guests. He invited me up by saying, "Come on in man, we don't smoke ci-gars we smoke ni-gars."

Part of playing the hand you're dealt is picking up the cards. Working in corporate America for 14 years, I saw and experienced enough inequities to last several lifetimes. My colleagues and I would routinely discuss how unfair corporate life was. Broken promises regarding promotions, jobs given to people without going through the appropriate posting procedures, and tons of natural informal mentoring relationships among white co-workers were the norm. For the most part early on though, we did more talking about our issues than doing something about them. We stared at our cards rather than playing them.

As a diversity consultant, I travel to companies facilitating one-day to one-week diversity workshops aimed at helping participants excel in this ever-changing workforce. I also provide direction in how to play the corporate hands they've been dealt. During the sessions we discuss and participate in activities and exercises centered around: the workforce changing demographics; the Equal Employment Opportunity and Affirmative Action goals, laws and regulations; the impact that stereotypes, perceptions, values, beliefs and collusion have on workplace interactions, synergy and opportunities; the business reasons for managing diversity; and the significance of self-empowerment.

The self-empowerment discussion is invaluable because sometimes things happen to you that make your head spin more than Linda Blair's in *The Exorcist*. Just as *Monopoly*, *The Game of Life*, *Scrabble*, *Twister* and *Trouble* have survived over time, participants adamantly insist corporate games are still around. And like those board games, the corporate games too have been updated.

Initially, there's often more angry conversation about the cards that have been dealt than the actual playing of the cards. To help them play their hands and clear some of their corporate hurdles, I encourage session attendees to use these Jim's Gems:

Gem 1: Secure mentors and coaches (of all races, ages, ethnicities and backgrounds).

Gem 2: Become outstanding, invaluable, a specialist in your area, by getting additional licenses, experiences, certifications and coursework.

Gem 3: Build relationships and align yourself with the appropriate reference groups.

Gem 4: Work collectively with others to defeat unfair practices both in and outside the workplace.

Gem 5: Take risks.

Gem 6: Stop providing the ammunition (i.e., the "stuff" that sinks your corporate ship: inappropriate dress, poor punctuality and work habits, improper grammar, weak technology skills, sub-par presentation skills).

Gem 7: Learn and understand your organization's corporate culture.

Gem 8:   Gain exposure throughout the organization through projects, volunteerism and assignments.

Gem 9:   Be open to feedback, but know your limitations.

Gem 10:   Look for ways to reinvent yourself, and be very slow to play your age, gender, sexual orientation, race, class or disability card if things are not going your way.

Playing the hand you're dealt builds character and fulfills dreams. It also creates opportunities to acquire wisdom and experience so that you can mentor and coach others. Today, I live to help people create new and improved hands for themselves. The first instructions I give them are to pick up their cards, look at them, and then start playing: that's when the cards begin to change. I remind them that in this card game called life, we can't throw in our cards and hope we're dealt better ones next hand. There is no next hand.

Average: Complaining about the hand you're dealt. Only doing something about your situation when things are rock-bottom low.

Awesome: Being proactive and resilient; earnestly and consistently playing the hand you're dealt. Incorporating Jim's Gems into your routine.

EXTRA AWESOME GIFT

I'll never forget the day my dad walked my older brother and me out to the barn. It was the first time I'd ever seen my dad cry. Immediately, I knew something was wrong. David, my younger brother, was very sick. It was cancer. In his small, not fully developed five-year-old brain, a tumor the size of a grapefruit was growing.

Over the next three-and-a-half years, David had two brain surgeries, plus radiation and chemotherapy treatments before finally succumbing to the cancer at the tender age of 8 ½. Never once in that time did I hear him ask, "Why me? Why not some other kid?" Not once did my parents ask, "Why did this happen to our child?"

My family's strength during that time was amazing. My parents tried to make life as normal as possible for us. We did not have health insurance and we had little money. My mom had taken a leave of absence from work to care for David, and my dad was away from home a lot.

I did not recognize the significance of what transpired over those three-and-a-half years until much later in life. For many years, we didn't talk about David. As we got older, talking about him became easier; we did it more frequently. As I have matured and have reflected on that period in my life, I have realized that every time I come across a challenging situation, or every time I need a bit of additional strength, I think about David, and I think about my family. They are what get me through. I get strength from them. Knowing what we went through— realizing that my parents watched one of their children die, unable to do much about it—makes one of life's curve balls seem like child's play.

—Kim Schreck (Sacramento, CA)

Quickly turn to your Personal Awesome Action Plan Page (p. 237) and write the five "awesome actions" you're going to take as a result of reading this chapter. When you're finished, turn back to read more about what it takes to go from average to awesome!

17

GIFT

Sssshh…Listen to Your Own Advice

*Hallmark moments or tragic situations prompt me to take self-inventory
of who I am, what I have done and what I desire to accomplish
in life to become a better person.*

—*Michael Robinson (Philadelphia, PA)*

Hate is an extremely strong word.

My friend Jaia hates her job. Jaia often talks to me about how much she hates her job. I hate that Jaia still has that job. I hate hearing about the job. OK, that's enough hate for the next 50 years. I very seldom use the word hate.

Jaia and I were talking on the phone recently. Immediately after we moved past "Long time no hear," "It's been months," and "How have you been?" (I'm sorry to say we started into the other traditional aspect of our telephone conversations: talking about her dead-end job.) This was my fault, I guess. I had asked how things were looking on the job front…had she found anything new? And like a courtroom defense attorney who just heard an inconsistency in the prosecution's star witness's testimony during his line of questioning, Jaia pounced on this opportunity to return to her job pity-party mantra.

She told me she had quit, but that her boss wouldn't let her leave. "Your boss wouldn't let you leave?" I thought angrily to myself. I was furious. But I didn't say much. I bit my tongue. I had grown tired of giving advice that was seldom used.

My friends often have to hang in there during my motivational pep talks. Like a doctor who has a diagnosis or prescription for all of her friend's ailments, I have an inspirational thought or two or three or four for whatever is ailing them.

Jaia got off the hook easy this time. After two or three motivational sentences, I was ready to move on to the next topic of conversation. "You're telling me the same things I always tell my son," she said matter-of-factly.

"What did you say?" I asked, knowing exactly what she said, but wanting to hear her repeat it.

"You're telling me the same things I tell …," she said before not completing the sentence. "I need to listen to my own advice, huh?"

How many times have we told people how to clean their kitchens when our sinks are filled with dirty dishes? How often have we told others to clean their cars when our trunks are filled with junk? We can tell others what to do but stop there. What's more confusing is that we become miffed when they don't take our advice, taking their situation personally, but not caring that our own situation is still in peril.

 We have Ph.D.s in other people's business but need tutoring in our own.

What's that about?

Pat Harmon, my photographer, finally listened to her own advice and has been doing cartwheels ever since. Upon entering college she majored in Pre-Law. This was an impressive field, one that could help create a financially satisfying living, she rationalized. However, after determining that this major required too much reading and decision-making, focusing more on what's in one's mind rather than what's in one's heart, she switched to Human Development.

Her first jobs were of the office variety. The jobs were "mind-paralyzing," not providing the consistent challenge, sincere personal interactions and positive energy she sought. Relying on the special satisfaction she received from taking pictures of family and friends (and from taking pictures of the tall ships as they sailed along the Delaware River in the 1980s), Pat took up photography. It wasn't long before she realized the obvious: she loved taking pictures and she was extremely good at it. Pat had an uncanny talent for working with and bringing out the best in people and capturing their innermost essence on film. Not only did she take fabulous pictures, but she also doubled as a career counselor and therapist, giving plenty of advice and feed-back during the photo shoot on how her clients could grow their careers and change their lives by following their hearts.

After 15 personally but not financially satisfying years, she began to listen closely to the number of "friends" who told her she could never make a living on her own just by taking pictures. "Make it a hobby, but not a living," they told her. They made the case and provided the contract and she signed on the dotted line. Pat returned to the safety and predictability of the corporate office.

Though boring and professionally unfulfilling, the job was secure, providing trimmings and perks her photography business did not, namely benefits and a steady paycheck. Relying on all of the "wise counsel" she had received, Pat talked herself into the notion that she had burned out on photography. The naysayers' words and thoughts became the lens cap that blocked the power and beauty that emanated from her camera.

After marinating in a series of internal reflection workshops, teach-ers and inspirational books, Pat became camera-hungry again. She learned that she could not sell what she did not believe in—namely herself and her work.

During her first photography jaunt, Pat had played not to lose rather than playing to win, even though she could do breathtaking things with a camera. She had a gift! Her clients fed off her. When she was "present" her photography was awesome! When she wallowed in worry (bills and a lack of steady customers will do that to you) her photography was average.

She began to listen to her own advice. She followed her heart.

Pat threw away her lingering self-limitations and doubts like a parent throws away a stinky diaper and made an unfailing commitment and promise to herself and to her work. With a renewed drive and fire, she reopened her photography business and has been on a steady diet of extremely satisfied customers ever since. She says she's now in a zone!

Average: Being ready to give advice to others but not ready to follow the advice you furnish, for yourself.

Awesome: Listening to your own advice, then sharing your lessons with others. Knowing, however, that the true teacher encourages students to find the answers within themselves.

Make yourself a promise. Promise yourself that you are going to start listening to your own advice, from this point forward. You're going to begin listening to the powerfully directional words of wisdom you freely give others. Promise yourself that you're going to spend more time writing the script to your own movie rather than always trying to direct the movies of others. Hey, you have great advice. Listen to yourself! You always want other people to.

EXTRA AWESOME GIFT

I've learned to trust my intuition and common sense. Some of the most successful and truly happy people I know are not necessarily the most intelligent or the most educated. What these people do have in common is that they consistently trust their inner voice, and they never stop applying good old common sense to their problems, challenges and opportunities. When things are at their toughest, I find a quiet place, relax, and LISTEN to my inner wisdom...it has never steered me wrong. And when you find yourself so down in the details of a particular problem or challenge that you just can't seem to find the answer or make a decision, don't be afraid to step back, rise above all of the "noise" and ask yourself, "Does this pass my common-sense test?"

—Joe Sparacino (Philadelphia, PA)

Quickly turn to your Personal Awesome Action Plan Page (p. 237) and write the five "awesome actions" you're going to take as a result of reading this chapter. When you're finished, turn back to read more about what it takes to go from average to awesome!

18

GIFT

Have a Forgiving Spirit

I look for the goodness in others. I'm genuinely interested in others, and it's amazing how much I learn and grow just listening to and engaging with people.

—*Deloris Davis (Philadelphia, PA)*

I was helping my uncle carry a chair down the stairs and out the front door. We—my mother, brother and I—were moving. We were leaving my father.

My father had a couple of personalities. One was spectacular. He was the life of every party: witty, charismatic, charming, sensitive and poetic. I enjoyed sitting on the living room couch watching him and my mom jitterbug and bop during one of our family "get down" nights. Plus he could *sing*! I loved when he sang, "It's a beautiful morning, I think I'll go outside for awhile…" or "God didn't make little green apples, and it don't rain in Indianapolis in the summertime…" or "Fly me to the moon and let me play among the stars…" He taught me how to listen to a baseball game on the radio and keep the scorebook at the same time. My love of sports—that was my dad's doing also. We used to race (I never did win), play half-ball and fly kites. That dad, unfortunately, didn't show up enough.

His other personality would rear its ugly head after he spent time with his after-work buddies. Guzzling adult beverages was their pastime. After making his post-work pit stops, Dad would take the train home. Upon getting off the train, usually appearing very disheveled, he would stagger down the street heading to our home on Sansom Street. The five-minute walk would take him what seemed like hours. From the living room window, I would dejectedly and somberly watch him stagger home. My friends, outside playing, would watch too. They would later do their "Jim's dad drunk-walking down the street" impersonations when we played.

The times he couldn't get his key in the door he'd ring our doorbell—until it stopped working. Then he'd just bang on the door with his fist. When he did manage to get his key in the door, he sometimes would come in and sit on the first step; we lived on the second floor of the apartment building. He would take a nap that lasted until the next morning, when it was time for him to go to work again. Other times, he would come upstairs, go straight to the bathroom and spend the night sleeping on the toilet. Those times when he successfully scaled the 14 steps that led to the hallway, he would, without fail, head to the living room looking behind the sofa, chair and television set for the bottles of beer, vodka and/or whiskey that he had hidden. Mom had usually found them first and had flushed them down the toilet. As regular as clockwork, that generally led to an extremely loud argument that at times turned physical.

As I was carrying the chair, I thought about when Mom first told us we were moving. She called my brother and me into the dining room and said, "I have $2100. We can use this money to buy a house that I've found or we can buy a new car." I asked my mom if we bought the new house was Dad going to go with us? She said no. My brother and I hesitated for a moment and then said, "Let's buy the house." The plan began.

We decided to move while my father was still at work. Since missing a full day of school wasn't an option, Rodney and I would get an early dismissal. My mom would take the day off from work to pack and we would be gone before my dad got home from work. I replayed all of this in my head as my uncle and I carried the chair down the steps.

When we reached the bottom step to head out the front door to the moving van, my dad met us. When I looked up he was directly in front of me. I was as motionless as a mannequin. Angrily he asked, "Where's your mother?" I looked down. "Where's your mother, Jimmy, what's going on? What are you doing?" Staring at the ground, I mumbled, "We're moving, Daddy, and Mom is upstairs in the kitchen." This was a rare day when Dad had not stopped off on the way home to hang out with his friends. Actually, he had left work early, hoping to spend some happy, quality time with his family. There was no sign of alcohol, just the handsome, concerned husband and father of two, James Alvin Smith, Sr.

He looked around for a quick second, assessing everything that was going on in front of him and immediately turned around. He walked down the front steps, around the corner and out of my life. In the next 25 years I saw my dad only a handful of times.

I carried a grudge every day for nearly a quarter of a century.

I played Little League sports. I played sports in high school. I played sports in college. I had several professional football tryouts. No dad to cheer me on. No dad to say, "That's my son!" No dad to break me down, then build me up. No dad to walk the sidelines, giving the coach "You better put my son in the game" looks. No dad to teach me the tricks of the athletic trade. No dad to talk to about relationships, the birds and the bees and love. No dad to teach me how to drive. No dad to go fishing with. No dad at my high school graduation. No dad at my college graduation. No dad when I received my Master's degree. No dad at my wedding. No dad at my daughter's birth. My mother wore both hats and I love her for that. I guess that's why I have a soft spot for single parents.

I did visit my dad once shortly after we moved. I went to the house after school to check in on him. It was a brief visit because he said he was heading out; my intuition told me that he wasn't ready to talk about things just yet. I still remember seeing his milk carton, water bottle and other groceries sitting on the windowsill between the screen and storm windows. Because we had taken the refrigerator, this was his makeshift method for keeping his food fresh. Mom gave him our new address and he actually stopped by a couple of times with toys, apologetic conversation and a plea to us to get Mom to take him back. The last time I saw him after that was when he stood on the sidelines, for the first and only time, during one of my Little League football games. What threw me was his traveling companion—a baby boy who I would later find out was my stepbrother, Mark. As the game wound down I looked to the sidelines for my father. I had hoped to receive some post-game, fatherly feedback. We'd gotten crushed, but I had returned a kickoff for a touchdown. Besides, it was the first time he'd seen me play organized football—uniforms, referees, the whole bit. He had gone.

During the next 20-plus years, I thought about trying to find him to clear the air, to let bygones be bygones. I discovered that he had remarried and that in addition to Mark I had a stepsister named Stacy. Stacy was his wife's daughter. I also learned that my dad still lived in Philadelphia, financially just making it from one day to the next, paycheck to paycheck.

We did walk into the same house a couple of times during family gatherings. We would stare at each other from a distance, looking more for the effects of time and age, never sharing more than a sentence or two. I had become resentful. Our communication consisted of a phone conversation every four or five years. He needed a S.W.A.T. team to get into my heart. When he had a mild heart attack, then later a stroke, I, along with Mom and Rodney, went to see him in the hospital. Once we saw that he was going to be fine, we hugged, shook hands, and I departed.

I saw him two other times. Once, I traveled to his West Philadelphia home to introduce him to my first wife on our way to an event in the same neighborhood. That awkward visit lasted approximately 30 minutes as I facilitated the meeting so that he conversed more with her than with me.

Five years later, when Daecia was born, I took my little angel and Pat to see him for the first time. Daecia was his first grandchild and he was thrilled to see her. I gave him her photo and he promised to stay in touch. The next time we talked, nearly three years later, he called to borrow $100. I mailed him the money, he returned it as promised and months elapsed before we talked again. After several more calls over a period of months, we agreed to meet for dinner to have a long-antici-pated heart-to-heart discussion about our past and our future. Like many of our planned get-togethers, the meeting never took place.

On the morning of our scheduled dinner meeting, my father had a heart attack at work and died. At age 59, James A. Smith, Sr. became a more painful memory for me than he ever had been before.

Dad's boss had driven him to work that morning, arriving around 6:00 AM. Dad was the custodian for a hair salon. When he realized he had forgotten his lunch, his boss volunteered to drive back home to pick it up. When the boss returned, approximately three hours later, he found my father slumped on the floor. My brother, who was contacted first, called me with the news. I was paralyzed, humbled and ached all over. I cried. I was really fatherless now.

Those many years of resentment and anger seemed so frivolous. Why hadn't I patched things up? Why hadn't I let go of my bitterness? Why hadn't I just been able to move on? Why couldn't I just have appreciated the fact that I did have a father and worked to develop some semblance of a relationship? Why hadn't I cultivated a forgiving spirit? When I sat inches away from his open coffin during the funeral and then again when I closed the furnace door during his cremation, I was totally distraught, blaming myself for this somber reconciliation. Yes, many people told me that he could have tried to find me, too. But I own a significant piece of that father-son relationship pie, and it still doesn't taste good.

After my father died, I decided that I wanted to do something note-worthy to honor his memory. Both through his charm and personality and through his battle with alcohol, nicotine and anger, he taught me how to be a man, how to be responsible and how to be a father. Yes, HOW to be a father.

 You can be a role model by teaching someone through your magnificence or through your miscues.

My father's death smacked me with the reality that you should live each day to the fullest because tomorrow is not promised.

I decided to start using "Jr." after my name. For the first 38 years of my life I was called James Smith, Jimmy Smith or Jim Smith, but never Jim Smith, Jr. So after May 9th, 1999, I began taking my father, through the use of "Jr.," everywhere I went. It was a minute gesture that turned into a wonderful tribute to the man I now think about every day. As a speaker, I'm introduced or I have the opportunity to introduce myself quite often. Now, in front of audiences of all sizes, I walk to the front of the room with my dad's memory in my head and in my heart.

How many people have you not forgiven? How many grudges are you tightly holding on to? How many people do you refuse to call because of something silly that happened 17 years ago? The life meter is always ticking. Life is gone way too soon. Why is it so difficult to have a forgiving spirit?

It's so easy to stay angry. It's even easier to keep one's distance. We always think that there will be more time. "One day," "Some day," and "We'll see," turn into "I wish," "I should have," and "Why didn't I?"

There's another piece to the Jim Smith, Sr. story that relates to forgiveness. I had to check myself again, this time because of my friends' absence at the funeral. As I sat staring into the coffin, wiping away my tears, I thought about my father's past and our spotty rela-tionship. From time to time, I looked into the crowd of supporters, searching for my family and my friends' comforting eyes. My family was there but, for a variety of reasons, many of my close friends were absent, save Paul Kallmeyer. Paul, one of my Titans, became one of my closest friends during our corporate days. He was also extremely helpful to me during my divorce. He became my confidant, my rock and my means for just kicking back.

My emotions continued to get the best of me. The realization that my father was gone hurt immensely. "There was so much I could have done," I thought to myself. I was a mess. I remember Paul walking over to me some time during the viewing, bending over to kiss me on the cheek, and telling me that everything was going to be all right. Actually, I was surprised that he was there. I really did not expect him to make it. He had just found out about my father's death a couple of days before the funeral. Plus, he had to drive nearly two hours to get there from his home. My dad's service was held in a neighborhood reminiscent of many depicted in movies portraying lower-class black urban life. Paul, who is white, really stood out. His being there will stay with me forever. To think that the only close friend of mine (my brother and I do have common friends who were in attendance) to attend would be my tall, white-lawyer, softball teammate and friend was befuddling but memorable. I was thankful for the many cards and flowers I received, yet I wondered why more of my other close friends were not there.

Initially I was disappointed. Then I intentionally lost touch with many of them for awhile. My father's death, however, would help to create a valley of space in my heart for forgiveness. I let it go. Later, I never mentioned anything to any of them about how I felt. Why take them there again?

Today we get furious with people when they change their minds. We get violent when motorists cross in front of us on the highway. We become enraged when someone hangs up the phone on us. We go bonkers when shoppers have more than the required number of items in their shopping cart in the express lane. Where's our forgiving spirit? Why do we become so angry? Why do we take things so personally? Why not empower ourselves to become steadfast in the face of adversity?

Average: Harboring resentment toward and disassociating yourself from those who disappoint you.

Awesome: Developing an incredible, forgiving spirit; not carrying personal disappointment and baggage around like a bad habit. Soliciting help from your Titans to help you unload your baggage. Writing, in your journal, your forgiveness and action steps for mending the fence.

I remember reading the following in the *Autobiography of Jackie Robinson: I Never Made It:*

"I have memories. I remember standing alone at first base—the only black man on the field. I had to fight hard against loneliness, abuse, and the knowledge that any mistake I made would be magnified because I was the only black out there. I had to fight hard to become just another guy. I had to deny my true fighting spirit so that the noble experiment could succeed. When it finally did, I could become my own man; many people resented my impatience and honesty. But I never cared about acceptance as much as I cared about respect…"

Jackie Robinson was the epitome of a forgiving spirit, and you can be, too. A forgiving spirit means:

- Refraining from thinking that it's always all about you (see Gift 21).
- Allowing room for others to make mistakes.
- "Being the change we wish to see in the world." (Mahatma Ghandi)
- Owning your piece and not consistently holding others responsible for everything that's happened.
- Remembering that "great works are performed not by strength but by perseverance." (Samuel Johnson)

People who have moved from average to awesome have learned to forgive and move on.

EXTRA AWESOME GIFTS

I've found that having a forgiving spirit has been significant in my life. When I've been in situations where I've needed to forgive, I remember that our essence—which is what spirit is—is that we are all loving people. My ability to let go, choose love and move forward is a wonderful opportunity for me to connect with my core. These moments of forgiveness have changed who I am, what I believe and how I interact with others. I hope that my actions will inspire others to have a more forgiving spirit.

—*Janae Bower (Minneapolis, MN)*

When I think of forgiveness I immediately think of Anthony DeMello. In his book The Way to Love, *p.119, he writes: "Every time you find yourself irritated or angry with someone, the one to look at is not that person but yourself. The question to ask is not 'what's wrong with this person?' but 'what does this irritation tell me about myself?' First look into the very real possibility that the reason why this person's defects or so-called defects annoy you is that you have them yourself. But you have repressed them and so are projecting them unconsciously into the other...*

Another thing is also clear: You become irritated with this person because he/she is not living up to the expectations that have been programmed into you."

—*Maria Garaitonandia (Cuernavaca, Mexico)*

Quickly turn to your Personal Awesome Action Plan Page (p. 237) and write the five "awesome actions" you're going to take as a result of reading this chapter. When you're finished, turn back to read more about what it takes to go from average to awesome!

AWESOME REFLECTIONS PAGE...

GIFT

Remember That the Cure for the Pain is in the Pain*

There were times when my body was weak and not able to sustain me. I almost died and that's when I lost my fear of death and learned to live. I failed both personally and professionally, but I realized that I could persevere. There is nothing anyone can do to me that causes fear and that in turn allows me the freedom to do what I want to do.

—*Elizabeth Andrews (Clinton Township, MI)*

My father introduced me to this theory when I was a little boy. To make sure that he had my full attention during our "character developmental" sessions he used a black or brown leather belt as his visual aid. Before he commenced these lessons of "appropriate home and school comportment, responsibility and discipline," he would passionately utter the phrase, "this is going to hurt me more than it's going to hurt you." I did not believe him then but I do now. Through my 43 years, I've learned some of my best lessons in life through pain, albeit emotional and psychological pain, *not physical.*

Why does emotional and psychological pain have to hurt so much? Why does it have to feel like our insides are being stretched from Connecticut to Cancun? Why does the pain have to linger like crumbs at the bottom of a toaster? Why does it have to prey on our minds incessantly? To remind us...to remind us...to remind us, to never again do what caused it.

*Taken from Roberto Almanzan's poem used in the video "Color of Fear," Stir Fry Productions 1994.

Pain has no prejudice and doesn't play favorites. All people experience hurt. Unfortunately, some people have to experience excruciating hurt and pain before they seek change.

It's why some children have to touch the fire to understand that fire will burn you. It's why some students have to take a 1.0 grade-point average home with them after their first semester to understand that if they don't thoroughly apply themselves as college freshmen they will invariably spend the next three-and-a-half years playing catch-up—if they don't flunk out. It's why some employees have to get fired to realize that inappropriate workplace behavior will not be tolerated. It's why some people have to catch their best friends talking behind their backs before they reevaluate their friendships. Life teaches us a lesson every day.

Granted, some of the lessons are more painful than others, but the end result for many is that we focus on the pain, rather than on the lesson and the action step we could take. And if the pain isn't intolerable, and we flunk the lesson, we usually venture right back into the same "pain game."

Our threshold for pain is unbelievable. That's why many of us stay in agonizing relationships and tormenting work situations. We hold on, hang on, latch on, and clasp on to whatever is causing our misery. One of my favorite inspirational stories is motivational speaker Les Brown's tale about the dog on the nail:

A father walks his son to school every day. And every day they pass a dog that is lying on a porch. What makes this particular dog different than other dogs in the neighborhood is that this dog is yelping, groaning, crying—obviously in some pain.

Well, father and son walk past the same dog on the same porch every day. Finally, one day, the little boy asks his father if he knows what's wrong with the dog. The father nods yes, saying that he has a pretty good idea what is causing the dog so much pain. He explains to his son that the dog is crying because he is lying on a nail.

Stunned, the little boy asks his father why doesn't the dog just get up off the nail? The father replies that the nail must not hurt the dog enough yet.

Isn't that just like us humans? We moan, groan, cry and complain to anyone in earshot. And if you're not in earshot, we e-mail you or call you on the phone. Some of us even develop a contingent of groupies and frequent criers who, without fail, show up to hear our monologues. If the price of admission were sound advice and resources, rather than B.Y.O.D. (bring your own drama), attendance would quickly dwindle. Most times we exhaust more energy in talking about the pain than we do eliminating its source. For a litany of reasons including fear, timing, guilt and lack of courage, we don't get off of our nails. As students of life, we fail to take copious notes about the painful lessons we're being taught, and we don't move on.

If we sit up straight, clear our minds and pay close attention to what's going on around us, we can learn plenty about ourselves and about others. We can learn from the broken promises, the divorces, the firings, the punishments, the disappointments, the bankruptcies, the promotion denials, the ruined friendships and runner-up finishes. Through these trials, we can learn to stop putting ourselves in certain situations, hopefully mustering the much-needed strength to incorporate into our lives the four Cs of Change: Commitment, Consistency, Courage and Confidence.

We can learn who brings out our Dr. Jeykll and who brings out our Mr. or Mrs. Hyde. We can learn to love ourselves so much that we will STOP starring in reruns of those morbid shows, stop repeating patterns of pain.

Some pain, however, a different kind of pain, catches us off-guard. Life doesn't always provide planning and preparation for pain. Life isn't fair that way. And for two of my friends, a type of pain in which they had no control, slid in totally unexpectedly four years ago, changing their lives forever.

Bill and Lynne Hart both had prosperous careers and "on the side" hobby/business pursuits to stay busy, happy, centered and connected to the community. They also had a growing, positive, always-smiling and ambitious teenager, Kelby.

Bill arrived home one evening and made a beeline to the backyard to get the dog and take him on their daily pre-evening, clear-your-mind, man-and-his-dog walk. Lynne was in the kitchen preparing dinner and Kelby was upstairs completing his homework.

Returning from the walk, Bill, put the dog back in the yard and called for Kelby to come down and fill him in on his school day. Wearing only his blue and gold University of Michigan basketball trunks and sneakers, Kelby raced down the stairs to greet his father.

Since Bill knew that Kelby had taken his pre-season physical for football that day, he quickly cut to the results after small talk about school. Kelby said that he had failed the physical because his knee was still banged up from a previous fall. However, the spirited 14-year-old said, loud enough so that his mother could hear him in the kitchen, "That's OK. I'm still 5'5 ½", and 125 pounds!" "I'm 5'5 ½", 125 pounds! I'm taller than you mom!" Bill smiled, looked at his son and began to talk about getting his knee looked at so that he could join the team soon.

Before Bill finished his next sentence Kelby fell back on the floor, unconscious. Bill yelled for Lynne to come into the room! She called the ambulance as he frantically tried to bring Kelby to. Desperately, Bill attempted mouth-to-mouth resuscitation and CPR, but to no avail. The ambulance arrived and Kelby was whisked to the hospital.

A few hours later, Kelby died of natural causes. Fourteen years old, 5'5 ½", 125 pounds. It was going to be difficult for Bill and Lynne to find the cure for their pain in this pain.

I went to visit them recently to interview them for this book. When Bill met me at the door, his face and a comment under his breath signaled that he had forgotten about our meeting. He had made other plans. I told him that we could reschedule and that I would come back another time. But he insisted that I come in and at least get a tour of the house. I greeted Lynne with a warm hug and then Bill turned into Julie McCoy (i.e., star of TV's *The Love Boat*), giving me my tour of the "Hart estate."

From bathrooms to bedrooms, sitting rooms to antique rooms, reflection rooms to eating rooms, I saw everything, save Kelby's room. Pointing to the white, closed door, Bill showed me where Kelby's room (still exactly the way Kelby had left it) was, but we did not go in. We stopped in Bill's third floor, memorabilia room, a shrine to Muhammad Ali and vintage jazz, when he began to talk about Kelby. He started by sharing how Kelby used to sneak into their bedroom in the morning to get Bill's cologne to wear. Bill laughed, as he told the story, adding that he had gone into Kelby's room that morning to put on his son's prized CK cologne.

Laughter turned to tears as Bill recounted the story to me, moment by moment, second by second. He squeezed his work tie in his hand as if he were holding Kelby's hand for the last time. My powerful friend missed his son dearly. He said that he and Lynne now take one day at a time, that some days are harder than others. They keep reminding themselves, that, "It is what it is and it can be no other way."

I was paralyzed. Bill was in tears. I kept thinking about Kelby's last words, "I'm 5'5 ½", 125 pounds!"

Honoring his time and wanting to make the tears go away, I said to Bill that he better get ready to head out. We hugged and returned downstairs. I said goodbye to Lynne, thanking her for permitting me to share Kelby with you. Within seconds, as she thought about her departed angel, she began to cry. "We're dealing with it Jim…he was such a sweet kid…I miss my baby," she said as I headed to the front door. I drove home pondering the life-altering journey I had been on ever since I started writing this book.

Bill and Lynne smile a lot these days. They are best friends. Their relationship is fabulous. They provide a consistent supply of love and support for each other. Kelby's memory will forever be in their souls. His pictures are in every room. But knowing Bill as I do, I know Kelby's memory fuels his drive to create awesome lives for those he touches. As both Bill and Lynne will tell you, "It is what it is and it can be no other way."

Average: Finding yourself in the same or similar painful situations over and over again.

Awesome: Learning from the painful situations and lessons that come your way and using these learnings to create powerful, positive differences in your life. Resolving, then putting into motion, behavior changes that suggest that you will not dive into your pain again, no matter how tempting it may be.

Bill and Lynne have managed a way to deal with their pain. However, the pain resulting from such a tragedy, and the kind of lessons learned, are quite different from the pain and lessons resulting from broken promises, divorces, firings, etc., which are situations we contribute (to a greater or lesser extent) and which we can learn to avoid. However, there's a blessin' in every lesson.

Awesome people have accumulated, and have learned from, myriad life lessons. They do see the blessin'. Through these lessons they've learned to toughen their resolve. Some of the lessons were pleasurable while others were excruciatingly painful. Pay attention, listen closely: sometimes the cure for the pain is in the pain.

EXTRA AWESOME GIFTS

I am learning to "be" with whatever is happening in my life—good and not so good. To feel pain is as human as feeling joy—to feel anger is as essential as feeling compassion. To avoid any emotion is to omit an essential piece in the mosaic of life. We did indeed learn these same lessons as children learning to cross the street: stop, look and listen...

—Judy Chapman (Toronto, Canada)

On the outside, people in my life saw me as a confident, talented winner, the kind of person who was good at everything she tried: school, sports, various jobs. They didn't see that on the inside, I was slowly becoming more and more obsessed with perfection; I was driven by a fear I couldn't name. I felt like everything out of my mouth was an excuse. If something went wrong, I could not admit to a mistake. I had to collect the evidence of perfection, but I didn't know what I was trying to prove. I felt like I was on trial for my life, but I didn't know why.

The fear and stress of perfectionism drove me to the edge of the cliff and I finally let someone see my pain. She asked me, "What's the worst thing that could happen if you make a mistake?" I realized that in my heart I believed that if I were wrong, I would be seen as a bad person. That would break my heart and I just couldn't bear it. I had to let go. It wasn't that I changed my mind; my mind was changed.

Afterward, when I made a mistake, I learned to admit it and saw that the world did not crumble as a result. In fact, I've come to believe that mistakes are the building blocks of excellence, allowing the mind and body to find the best approach by eliminating the ones that don't work. All those years I had been robbing myself of the very thing that would really move me toward my full potential. Today, perfection isn't good enough for me.

—*Shannon Percy (Minneapolis, MN)*

Quickly turn to your Personal Awesome Action Plan Page (p. 237) and write the five "awesome actions" you're going to take as a result of reading this chapter. When you're finished, turn back to read more about what it takes to go from average to awesome!

GIFT

Start With the Wing First!

When you find yourself overwhelmed, I suggest that you keep it simple.
Narrow your focus to the things you can control and the outcomes you
want to achieve. Approach all of the other variables with flexibility and
a positive attitude. Also avoid beating yourself up
if things don't go 100% as planned.

—Laura Bruner (Austin, TX)

When was the last time you plopped down at the dinner table, starving, impatiently waiting for someone to bless the food? Before the prayer, you scanned the table to see how you were going to pile and position everything onto your plate when something voluminous caught your eye: at the end of the table was a plump, mouth-watering, perfectly seasoned, stuffed turkey.

Do you recall the time when the only thing that stood between your appetizer and your dessert was a delicious, eight-hour marinated, golden-brown baked chicken-guarded by brown rice and grilled vegetables? Just thinking about those two meals makes me hungrier than a famished, frustrated dieter after a Jenny Craig dinner.

Nevertheless, if one of those two entrees were in my knife and fork's immediate consumption range, I would not pretend to be a Pac man with a screen full of dots. Common sense and eating decorum would prevail. I would nonchalantly cut off the wing, then the drumstick, then some of that scrumptious white meat. I can almost guarantee, though, like a patron at an all-you-can-eat buffet, I would return for second and third helpings, but it would be done in good taste—and it would taste good too!

You're probably asking yourself, "How do these feasting tips relate to moving from average to awesome?" Hang in there my friend…I'm going to feed your interest.

When your problems, concerns or "to-do's" lie before you with all the variety and expansiveness of a Thanksgiving feast, why don't you wade through them one at a time: wing, then drumstick, then thigh? Like impatient people who dump salt and pepper on their food before they've even tasted it, some people attempt to consume their entire "to-do" list or stack of problems all at once. Any dietitian or psychologist will tell you that you can get sick that way.

The insanity-inducing scenarios usually play out as follows. We either: (1) assess all that's in front of us and then become overwhelmed, complaining to others how much we have to do; (2) assess all that's in front of us, make a to-do list, then remain immobilized with a severe case of paralysis by analysis; or (3) dejectedly assess all that's in front of us, begin attacking everything at once, become frustrated because nothing gets thoroughly accomplished, then have another pity party about everything that remains on our plate. Then, before we can even see the white of our plate, we volunteer for and take on more stuff. And during all of this shuffling, hustling, and running around, life leaves more poop on our doorstep.

People who have moved from average to awesome optimistically start with the wing first.

Many time-management experts would disagree however, citing the merits of aggressively wrapping your arms around the most difficult or challenging item on your list first. Save the smaller items to be the bread that soaks up the gravy, mussel sauce and crumbs that remain on your plate, they insist. I don't know about others, but I relish getting little wins under my belt first, building up a head of steam and some momentum. When I have multiple tasks in front of me, I assess my list, prioritize, and then get busy. And getting busy means generally picking some of the low hanging fruit (i.e., the wing) first, then moving on to weightier tasks.

We become so frazzled when we think that we're carrying the entire world on our shoulders. We feel beat down, exasperated, put upon. But it's an all-too-familiar feeling. Whether they're work-related issues or home-based horror stories, our "feeling overloaded" complaints are innumerable. After awhile we begin to sound the same. That's why people stop listening to us.

Unfortunately, tackling overflowing "to-do" lists is not the only way we subject our resolve to a stress test. Consider those instances when we seek to make professional and personal life changes. We read books (like this one); listen to self-help tapes and CDs; seek guidance and direction from friends; watch inspirational, educational infomercials or television shows on PBS; and attend motivational speaking events. However, similar to the way we handle our piles of professional and personal laundry, we move hastily, putting into motion plans for three thousand life-altering changes in five minutes. That's more pressure than rushing to the airport in a city you're unfamiliar with, with a drop of gas left in your rental car gas tank, to catch your flight (the last one of the night).

There's a better way. When the hills of pressures and tasks get so high that you need a trampoline to see over them, or when you're about to make significant life changes, TAKE AN EXTREMELY DEEP BREATH, AGAIN, AGAIN, then start with the wing first. Incorporate these 10 steps:

1. Make a list of everything you want to do, then prioritize your list.

2. Take time to visualize yourself accomplishing everything and how you're going to feel when the tasks are complete.

3. Next to each "to-do," list a time frame, an action (i.e., how you're going to do it), tools or resources you're going to need and a measurement (i.e., how will you know when that task is completed).

4. List those people whom you'll get to assist you.

5. Make a plan "B" list as well. In the event your plan "A" doesn't work, you will need a back-up.

6. Determine how you're going to reward yourself once you've completed half of your list and how you're going to reward yourself when your list is totally accomplished.

7. Begin with several less complicated tasks or changes that you can execute quickly. That will help you build momentum and positive energy.

8. Finally, vigorously go after your other priorities, one at a time.

9. When Mrs. Doubtfire, Brother But and Sister Settle start to visit your subconscious, consider the consequences of not completing your assignment. Then just do it.

10. Maintain an extremely positive outlook the entire time. Don't waver, regardless of how things may seem. If you run into a rut, reread Chapters (Gifts) 3, 4, 5 and 6 of this book. Envision yourself winning! Envision yourself getting through the piles! Envision yourself at that new place–the new, more empowered and less emotionally drained you, minus the entire residue of the past.

I create lists nearly everyday. My lists are my security blankets. However, regardless of how many tasks I include, I start with the wing first.

EXTRA AWESOME GIFT

One of the things I do is focus on what I want to create in my life instead of focusing on what hasn't worked or what might not work. I think of what I want, and then I work toward achieving that. When "deficit" thinking starts to occur, I talk about it—either to confidants who I know will not simply indulge in my "pity party" or to someone who I know will have a perspective that will keep me balanced. I also do self-talk where I say to myself: "So what's this about?" "Why are you going there?" "What are you going to do about it?"

—*Deloris Davis (Philadelphia, PA)*

Average: Trying to accomplish everything (work, home, personal changes, etc.) at once. Becoming overwhelmed by the number of tasks that await you.

Awesome: Developing a driven, committed, disciplined disposition and approach to handling the number of challenges and tasks that greet you everyday. Maintaining that same approach, resourcefulness and resiliency when it involves making personal life changes.

Quickly turn to your Personal Awesome Action Plan Page (p. 238) and write the five "awesome actions" you're going to take as a result of reading this chapter. When you're finished, turn back to read more about what it takes to go from average to awesome!

21

Know That It's Not Always All About You

---

*What "gets me up" is my dedication to help others discover
more of who they are. Helping others connect what they believe to what
they say and do is my motivator.*

—Renee Gallart (New Hope, PA)

The clock—tick, tick, tick—was winding down to the finish. Less than
four minutes remained in the game. Mr. Momentum had changed
sidelines and was now proudly wearing Widener blue and yellow. My
teammates and I were eagerly and confidently inching closer to winning
the 1981 Division III National Football Championship in the Amos
Alonzo Stagg Bowl. The Dayton Flyers were scrambling to regain the
lead they had held so comfortably for three-and-a-half quarters.

Dayton had the ball on its own 25-yard line, but we had the lead,
14-10. It was an ironic scenario, promising to provide some poetic
justice, for this was the long-anticipated rematch of the previous year's
semifinal thriller, which Dayton had convincingly won 28-24, over-
coming a 24-0 half-time deficit. They won the National Champion-
ship in their next game while we soaked our injuries and made excuses
for what could have and should have happened.

I played right defensive cornerback. I looked over to their side-
line before going to our huddle to see if I could determine what play
they were going to run next. With my eyes fixated on their coach, I

determined what the play was going to be. The receiver was going to run approximately 10 yards, stop, fake right then turn left, looking to catch the pass that should already be in flight. Dayton was going to run the play right in my direction! I was so confident that I knew what was coming, I never did report to our makeshift huddle to hear the defensive call.

My mind raced as I waited during those precious few seconds before the play unfolded. I determined that: I would make the interception and race the 35 or so yards down the field untouched for the touchdown.

Once in the end zone I would: (1) take off my helmet and graciously smile for the camera, (2) say "hi" to my mother, Rodney and other family members, (3) do some sort of commemorative dance reminiscent of the Soul Train dancers and (4) jump into the arms of my jubilant teammates who would join me, within seconds, in my jubilant end zone celebration.

I was Walter Mitty in a football uniform.

I did have the play called right. The receiver ran about eight yards in my direction, but he failed to fake, heading directly to the sideline to make the reception and get out of bounds. This was even better than I had dreamed. "Professional football and highlight reels here I come," I thought as I moved to catch the brown, leather spiral heading in my direction. I ran and then leaped for the ball as it headed directly toward my outstretched arms. For a fraction of a second I took my eyes off of it to see if my path to a National Championship ring, the cover of Sports Illustrated and an end zone celebration was still clear. I saw nothing but pristine, green grass. When I looked up again I watched the ball sail through my fingers.

I dropped the ball!

I dropped the ball!

I dropped the ball!

Widener won the game 17-10. I did receive my National Championship ring. But more than that, I learned a couple of lessons: (1) it's not always all about me and (2) not everything is always going to go as planned, but can still work incredibly well.

Earlier in the game I had made the key block that enabled our punt returner, Tom Deery, to race 76 yards for our first touchdown and begin our comeback. It was a significant contribution to our winning the game, but not the way I had envisioned making the highlight reel. I wanted to score the winning touchdown. I wanted to make THE big play. I wanted to be on *The Tonight Show*. I wanted to be the star of the game. I wanted the reporters around my locker after the game. I wanted to get to the team bus late because autograph seekers were hounding me like paparazzi at a celebrity's wedding.

Don't be misled; I was ecstatic that we won. We finished the season 13-0. In silent prayer I thanked God and briefly reflected on our accomplishment, then jumped on the pile of giddy Widener football players celebrating in the middle of the field. Nevertheless, while flying back to campus that evening I looked out the airplane window, staring, searching into the darkness. While my teammates made enough noise to conjure up thoughts of every January 1 at 12:00 AM, I tried to figure out how and why I had dropped that pass.

I wanted my championship game experience to be special, like so many other memories in my sports past. I always scored the winning basket or got the key hit. I wanted more than simply playing in the game or making a key block, which to my mind were like making the lemonade or bringing the charcoal to the family reunion: important—maybe even essential—but not at all glamorous or noteworthy. I wanted the Oscar for *Best Leading Man in a National Championship College Football Game*, not best supporting actor.

Fast forward to now. That lesson is etched in my mind. You can play a powerful role in any endeavor without always having to be the star. (Still, if I had a chance to do it all over again, I would have caught the interception, scored the touchdown and hoped that life would serve up another opportunity for me to learn that awesome lesson. Just kidding…I think.)

Playing Robin to someone else's Batman is not the easiest occupation, especially when Batman doesn't send any credit your way. Haven't you seen entertainers fighting over the microphone to determine who was going to sing or talk? In the corporate training arena, I've seen professional trainers have egotistical moments, quarreling before, during and after sessions over who was going to facilitate the perceived most prominent segments of the workshop. I've seen speakers go way over their allotted presentation time because they reeked of "it's all about me."

Realizing that it's not always about you means being humble, self-sacrificing, confident, intuitive and gracious. Occasionally we need to be the learner, the listener, the student, the chorus–the Pips to Gladys Knight. There's so much we can gain by moving away from center stage.

I worked with one of my favorite clients not too long ago. My deliverables included facilitating a diversity train-the-trainer session on Wednesday and Thursday, then leading a half-day diversity session on the subsequent Tuesday morning. I usually fly home immediately after my work is completed, but this time, since I would be returning to the same client site in Chicago in a few days, I decided to stay over the weekend. That way I could save my client money by eliminating a roundtrip airfare; in addition, I wanted uninterrupted quiet time to work on this book. The initial manuscript was nearly complete and having Friday, Saturday, Sunday and Monday to apply the finishing touches seemed very appealing. I conjured up thoughts of completing my final thesis for my graduate school project at Temple. I took a week off from work and lived in the library. I read and typed, read and typed until my 90-page, single-spaced project was finished. Similarly, meals aside, I planned to stay in my hotel room until the manuscript was done!

Before I left the building on Thursday, however, my client, Tony Graham, asked me if I had any plans for Friday. I told him of my intention to go into seclusion with my manuscript and he laughed. He then dangled the big, fat, juicy carrot, the excuse that would alter my plans and provide another anecdote for this book. He said that the company was bringing in motivational speaker Les Brown to keynote at their national sales meeting in July. He said that he was going to watch Les give a motivational talk to a group of educators, then take him to lunch to discuss the July engagement. Then he dangled the carrot lower, right in my salivating face. He asked if I would like to join him. After taking a full thousandth of a second to think it over, I asked Tony what time he would be by in the morning to pick me up. He could have said 3:00 AM and I still would have been ready.

With regard to motivational speaking, I've admired Les' work for over 20 years. He was the measuring stick I used for other speakers, including myself. I'd seen Les speak numerous times, could recount many of his powerful stories and quotes, had bought his tapes and read his books. But I'd never been up close and personal with him.

I went to bed that night thinking, "I'm going to meet Les Brown, I'm going to meet Les Brown…he could certainly give my career a boost, assist with my book and my speaking." I dreamed of what gifts the next day would provide. I was going to meet the Michael Jordan, the Bette Davis, the Frank Sinatra, the Jesse Owens, the Josephine Baker, the Beethoven, the Picasso of motivational speaking. I wouldn't need to have the hotel call and wake me up in the morning. This career and life changing opportunity would be my wake-up call. I was meeting THE Motivator, the man who had taught me, albeit from a distance, the most about the rhythm, pace, movement, voice quality and other mechanics of motivational speaking.

Tony arrived at 6:00 AM. We drove 90 minutes to the school auditorium to watch Les do his thing. After nearly two hours of vintage Les, the attendees were ready to take on the world and I was ready to take Les to lunch.

Les joined us, and the three of us drove to the restaurant. With Tony behind the wheel and me behind Les in the passenger seat, I prepped to blitzkrieg Les with the 5,322 questions I'd waited nearly 20 years to ask. Then it hit me. This wasn't about me! This was about Tony, my client, securing Les Brown to speak at his key sales meeting. This was his meeting. Tony needed all of the precious time we had to question and connect with his speaker. As much as I wanted to take the microphone, I relented; I would sit on the bench during this game. In the car and during lunch, I listened, listened and listened, save for one brief moment in the car when Tony pulled over to ask for directions and Les asked me what was my claim to fame. In 30 seconds, I gave him a WOW that I'm sure would have made Lisa Nichols very proud (turn back to the Introduction to find out what a WOW is).

After his business conversation with Tony was over, Les turned the conversation to me. Taking advantage of my brief moment (my time was limited since Les' limousine was waiting out front to drive him to the airport), I was extremely intentional. I candidly and passionately shared my past but mostly my future, focusing primarily on this book and my motivational speaking pursuits. He listened intently, smiling, taking it all in. I could see his mind working. I sensed that we connected. He said I had a gift, that there was something special about me. With that, he gave me his home phone number, asked if he could write the foreword for the book you're now reading, and headed to the car. Partially stunned, I stopped him to see if he was serious or if I was just hearing things. He did not blink, saying he would be honored. What a moment!

I learned plenty just by watching and listening to him during his conversation with Tony, a virtual needs-assessment meeting. My mind took thorough notes. I learned more by merely listening than I ever would have if I ran my mouth or competed with Tony for airtime.

As we drove back to my hotel, Tony thanked me for not interrupting him while he took care of his business. He said he really appreciated that I put my enthusiasm and my agenda on hold. I told him that I had learned a long time ago that it is not always about me.

A key ingredient to being awesome is realizing that it's not always about you. One of the ways you can demonstrate that is by helping other people become awesome. Tony's meeting conversation was more significant than my groupie adulations. Les and Tony had to connect in order for Les to have a successful keynote in July.

Freely give your time, resources and support to people who could benefit from your talents, wisdom and skills. My job has put me in a position to meet thousands of people. Many are craving for a timely word, a pat on the back, a vote of confidence or just a second of my time. You can become someone's Titan by volunteering your time or your energy, and by moving that spotlight in his or her direction. And if you really want to grow, then seek out opportunities to give, coach, mentor or assist people who are different from you. There are many in your professional and personal life who can benefit from your special skills, experiences and talents.

You have an awful lot to offer even if you have more yesterdays than tomorrows. We grow from our responses to people, projects, challenges and champions.

 Treat every day like you have not done your best work yet.

I am who I am largely because people saw something in me and decided to help fine-tune it, shape it and help others to benefit from it. Now I do the same and you can too. But to do so you have to remember that it's not always all about you.

Average: Solely focusing on your own agenda...what's in it for you. Always looking for opportunities to grab the spotlight or attention for yourself.

Awesome: Routinely looking for opportunities to help others. As a trainer or speaking professional, knowing that the most important people in the room are the people sitting in front of you. Sharing your skills, trade secrets and network of colleagues and friends. Truly being OK with not always having to be behind the steering wheel; actually seeking opportunities to steer the conversation in someone else's direction.

EXTRA AWESOME GIFT

The following is an article that was written, by Elmer Smith for the *Philadelphia Daily News* after the 2002 Academy Awards. The article discusses the epitome of selflessness. Read how some special actors demonstrated, through their giving, that it's not always all about them.

I didn't see Ossie Davis or Ruby Dee when the cameras scanned that glittering crowd at the Oscar ceremonies Sunday. Maybe I missed them. They aren't the kind who stand out in a 24-carat crowd. But I could feel them Sunday as Sidney Poitier, Denzel Washington and Halle Berry took turns accepting the accolades of their peers. I could feel Paul Robeson, Oscar Michaux, Hattie McDaniels.

And Steppin Fetchit.

"He was one of my heroes," Ossie Davis told me once, on a night I will never forget…a night that helped create a story about our responsibility to hold open those doors that someone held open or kicked down for us in whatever fields we labor in.

Denzel Washington and Halle Berry received the recognition that they earned through their own hard work and artistry. Nobody gave them anything. But they understood that they had crossed a bridge built by people who came before them and that it doesn't take anything from them to acknowledge that. That's why Denzel remembered Sidney Poitier and Halle Berry remembered Spike Lee. And that's why Ossie Davis remembered Steppin Fetchit on a night when my wife and I fawned over him and Ruby Dee.

This was nine years ago at the home of (friends) Larry and Larverne Depte… (who had developed a professional and personal relationship with the two movie greats). My wife and I jumped at the chance when the Deptes asked if we'd like to meet Ossie and Ruby at a small dinner party at the Deptes' home.

We talked about marriage—they had been married for 45 years at the time—and about the civil-rights movement, and their meetings with Malcolm X and Martin Luther King, Jr. When we finally steered the conversation around to their acting careers, I told them how much I admired them for refusing roles that would demean them or us. They shrugged it off. When I persisted, he told me why Steppin Fetchit was such an important pioneer.

Fetchit had made a career out of playing the foot-shuffling, head-scratching stereotype. Watching it used to make me cringe. I had always felt he sold us all out to get rich. Ossie Davis and Ruby Davis corrected me. He did what he had to do to get his foot in the door, Davis told me. And when he did, he held the door open for others like them. He knew exactly what he was doing and why he had to do it, Davis said. Steppin Fetchit shuffled his feet and scratched his head so we would only have to shuffle our feet, Davis said.

By the time we came along, Ruby Dee said, we could say, "OK, boss, I don't mind shuffling, but I won't scratch my head."

The black actors who followed them didn't have to shuffle or scratch their heads because someone else had already paid that price. It was paid by Oscar Michaux, a brilliant black filmmaker who had to accept the demeaning roles that were a black actor's staple so he could raise the money to make films that portrayed black families and individuals in ways that most America wasn't used to seeing us in.

Paul Robeson used to look so natural in bib-top overalls with a shovel in his hand that you could almost forget that he was a brilliant scholar who had earned a Phi Betta Kappa key at Rutgers University. There were others whose names wouldn't mean very much to you and me. I'm sorry I can't remember their contributions.

But they will never be forgotten—as long as people like Ossie and Ruby and Denzel and Halle can keep a foot in the door.

> *—Printed with Permission from the Philadelphia Daily News, Wednesday March 27, 2002.*

Quickly turn to your Personal Awesome Action Plan Page (p. 238) and write the five "awesome actions" you're going to take as a result of reading this chapter. When you're finished, turn back to read more about what it takes to go from average to awesome!

22 GIFT

Dance Like Nobody's Watching

Living the transformational life for the past eight months or so has been such a gift. Some call it the mid-life crisis. We can get so caught up in what others think of us—where we are personally and professionally. I call it transformation time and I love it. I'm moving! I'm growing! I'm dancing! It's so rewarding. I'm no longer looking for approval. Words cannot even describe the power.

—Rajean Bifano (Flagstaff, AZ)

Been to a wedding lately? Beautiful wedding party? How was the reception? Great food? How was the music? Did that person show up? What person, you ask? You know who I'm referring to—that "Gene, Gene, the Dancing Machine" person. He/she is that special, happy, outgoing, extroverted person who commandeers the dance floor. Others at the reception point and laugh at him, thinking that he is more inspired by adult beverage consumption than by the tunes emanating from the deejay's speakers.

But they're wrong; this person caught dance fever by simply deciding that he was going to have an awesome time. First it's the Electric Slide, then the Cha Cha Slide, the Macarena and the Twist. After the Chicken Dance, Shout, the YMCA, the Soul Train Line and other wedding-dance favorites, you can tell that he is just warming up. As you watch him in the Conga Line you can tell that he is in the ZONE, the dance trance, the party hearty pavilion. And guess what, he doesn't care who's watching.

Former baseball pitching great Satchel Paige provided one of my all-time favorite quotes when he described how he believed one should live his/her life. Paige said: *"Dream like you will live forever, work like you don't need the money, love like you have never been hurt and dance like nobody's watching!"*

Wow! What would happen if you could transfer that way of thinking to everything you do? What would happen if you lived as if nobody was watching, unconcerned about:

- consistently trying to please people;
- always asking for permission to do the simplest things;
- what management will say;
- wearing clothes that are in line with what others will be wearing;
- doing things the way they've always been done;
- whether your professor or teacher will grade you more for quantity than for creativity;
- how others receive your passion for…;
- how long it will take you to…;
- what others think about your potential or ability;
- being the first to start dancing at the party;
- doing everything exactly the "right way";
- whether you're following the exact steps others took to reach a goal.

Can you imagine that? We can be so driven by and so wedded to what others say and what others think that we don't let our genius, our creativity, our spontaneity or our true colors come out to play.

Our lives are so inundated with organizational and societal mores and norms that we seldom unleash our greatness, our power, and our gifts. That's what I hope you get from this discussion. This is not a rallying cry for being self-centered and selfish. Nor is it a call for reckless behavior. It's a cheer for being unique, being spontaneous, being in the moment, hearing the beat, then going for it without trepidation and regret.

Those times when you do let your hair down, don't you usually say at some point, "All right…that was fun! I need to do this more often." That's what I'm suggesting you do: do "it" more often. Soon "it" will become a part of you.

I started dancing like no one was watching in the 1960s when I would perform concerts in my bedroom with my brothers Jackie, Tito, Marlon, Jermaine and Michael. Yes, I was the sixth member of the fabulous Jackson 5 before Randy arrived on the scene. I'd play one of our many albums, position my G. I. Joes as audience members, put on one of my mother's huge Afro wigs, move my dresser mirror closer and dance and sing for hours. I knew every word to every song. Those moments have certainly played a role in shaping my creativity, my speaking, my training style and my free spirit.

How many people do you know who are so predictable they're boring? How many people do you know who don't get excited about anything, preferring to remain in a place of calm and casual reserve? Les Brown says that if you live your life being casual you'll become a casualty.

We become settlers. We settle for dead-end jobs. We settle for living in neighborhoods that drive us up the wall. We settle for relationships from which we don't grow. We learn to accept the circumstances we've been given. As a result, because we're afraid to take risks and we fear failure, driven by what others are going to say about what we do and how we do it, we live like somebody's watching all of the time. We don't hear the dance music.

It's as if we constantly need approval to flourish.

I rely heavily on the customer service I receive, especially considering my heavy travel schedule. If I had a brick for every person that has said to me, "Wait a second, I have to ask my manager if I could do that," or "That's not my job...I'm only the...," I would be able to build skyscrapers in all 50 states, and have enough bricks remaining to build a barbeque pit in every backyard in Philadelphia. And my requests are not that cumbersome. Can I have an extra one of those? Please remove this from my bill since I did not order that. Can you switch my room since this one has...? It's not until I drop the name of the company I'm representing that they jump. This gets tiresome fast.

It doesn't take a brain surgeon, Oxford Scholar or Ph.D. to determine that there are more people who don't dance like nobody's watching than those who do. Add to that the number of people who live their lives playing to keep the score close rather than to win and you have a Grand Canyon of unfulfilled people. This phenomenon rears its ugly head in many ways.

Certain ethnic groups, at times, seek safe careers historically germane to their culture because they think it's the appropriate, acceptable or preferred thing to do. Here comes the generalizations: Indian, medicine; Jewish, law protection; Irish, law enforcement. Some people are more driven by obtaining titles and labels (manager, vice president, doctor, esquire, supervisor, head this, head that) than obtaining happiness. Start setting and clearing your own personal achievement bar and stop worrying about what other people say or think. Put your energy where your dreams are.

Doing just that is how:

- Jim Hensen gave us the muppets;

- Dick Vitale gives us "Awesome Baby!";

- Wilma Rudolph and Flo Jo gave us Olympic records and gold medals;

- Flip Wilson gave us Geraldine;

- zany Dennis Rodman turned a mediocre basketball career into million dollar contracts, movies, wrestling matches, a best selling book and five NBA championship rings;

- Carol Burnett, Bill Cosby, Robin Williams and Whoopi Goldberg have made us laugh for years with their special brand of comedy.

If you make public or work-related presentations, stretch yourself. Dare to be different. There's too much D.B.P.P. (death by power point). Begin your presentation from the back of the room. Stand on a chair if it enhances your message and others' viewership. Raise your voice if it gets your message across better. Start your session with an activity rather than introducing the objectives first. Use more visuals—most people think in pictures rather than words anyway.

Be a walking, talking visual aid for living your dreams and for dancing like nobody's watching. You don't get in life what you want; you get what you are!

Oh, one more thing…stop laughing at the person dancing at the reception. Get up and join him/her! Now slide to the left. Slide to the right. Jump two times. Now give me some cha cha! You got it!

"It is far better to be free to govern, or misgovern, yourself than to be governed by anybody else."

—*Kwame Nkrumah*

"The impulse to dream had been slowly beaten out of me by experience. Now it surged up again and I hungered for books, new ways of looking and seeing."

—*Richard Wright*

Average: Settling for being just OK. Waiting for things or opportunities to knock on your door or to come your way. Through your behavior, seemingly asking for approval and permission to live or to perform your job. Being consumed with what others think of you.

Awesome: Unleashing your greatness and creativity. Taking risks and learning from them. Stretching yourself to be awesome, outstanding and happy. Getting on the dance floor first. Karaoke. Looking for fresh, new approaches. Living your dreams.

EXTRA AWESOME GIFT

You have to make it happen for yourself because nobody else will do it for you. You have to do what your heart tells you to. But that's a lot easier said than done.

After working as a manufacturer's sales representative selling wholesale to gift shops for about a year, making very little money (depending on the season), I knew I couldn't do this same job forever. I needed something more challenging and with more stability. I had been floating from one job to the next for four years.

After some long thought, I considered some sort of job working with children. At every party, I ended up playing with the kids or just talking to them. I often found children more stimulating and interesting than adults. I decided that before I made another job change I would take a graduate school course in Education. I was quite hooked on the idea of working with children, regardless of what others thought.

My next dilemma was that I was 27, without any formal or practical training in Education. How could I get a job teaching, even with a graduate degree in another subject area (I was finishing up my MBA), without any experience in the field of Education?

One day, after a HORRIBLE sales call, I drove from Cape May (NJ) to Blue Bell (PA) for a potential new account. Not only didn't they buy anything, I got a speeding ticket!

I then drove by a school. I circled the school twice, wanting to go in and inquire about teaching opportunities, but I started thinking about not having a degree in Education. Nevertheless, I finally pulled into the school parking lot and went in. I at least looked like I was ready for an interview, dressed in a sharp business suit, carrying a briefcase. I asked one of the office staff to see the principal but she just gave me the hairy eyeball and looked me up and down before answering. I explained to her that I was a grad student at

Cabrini College and was interested in volunteering or obtaining information about a part-time job.

Suddenly the principal popped up from behind the file cabinet with a guilty grin. He explained that it was common for parents to arrive this week, before school starts, to complain about their children's placement with a teacher. He thought that I was a bullet he should dodge. As fate would have it, he was also an adjunct professor at Cabrini and arranged for me to get an interview for a lunch aide job. I took the job on the remote chance I'd get an additional three-hours-a-day classroom aide job that, combined, would pay enough to help with my mortgage and some of my student loans.

Because of my dream to work with children, and by taking a risk to make it happen, and by not letting others' opinions become my reality, I ended up working at the same school throughout grad school as an aide. When I graduated I got a long-term substitute spot for a year, and then I got a contract for a permanent position. I've been feeling awesome ever since! I love being with children! And I don't care that it's not the perceived awesome sales job that others think I should have.

—Danielle Kallmeyer (Montgomeryville, PA)

Quickly turn to your Personal Awesome Action Plan Page (p. 238) and write the five "awesome actions" you're going to take as a result of reading this chapter. When you're finished, turn back to read more about what it takes to go from average to awesome!

GIFT

Listen to the Music

When things go wrong, don't go with them.
—*Les Brown (Potomac, MD)*

I've referred to movies several times in this book. Something happens during most movies to foreshadow or hint at what's going to occur next. Think about it. What happens during a movie that suggests something good, tragic, triumphant, grand, exhilarating, sad or momentous is going to happen? If you're thinking music, you're right. Whether it's fast, loud, up-tempo, inspirational, dramatic, slow or lovey-dovey, you can get a sense of what's about to occur from the music. The same thing happens in life.

We hear but we don't always listen to the music.

I used to work for a major bank in Philadelphia. One of the reasons I took the job was because it was my first opportunity to work in the city. This job helped move me closer to my roots, my mother (who worked across the street), my brother (who worked three blocks away), and my home. I was there for several months before I started to hear the music.

Mergers and acquisitions were being mentioned in the newspaper every day. Some huge company was always gobbling up some other smaller company. Or two powerhouses were joining forces to become Godzilla Goliath, Sr. And various banks, including my company, were always being mentioned.

The highest-ranking female executive, a person loved and admired by numerous people in the bank, left the organization. When she acknowledged that she was leaving to pursue other personal interests, I heard the music become louder.

The rumors in the banking industry that we were in play–meaning that other banks were considering acquiring us—wouldn't go away. The music got louder.

Other key management members left for "other opportunities." It was hard to hear myself think over the music.

The bank's CEO put an ad in the Sunday newspaper saying we would not be acquired. For me, that put the music at a fever pitch. Two weeks later we were sold. The music was deafening!

My greatest surprise was that nearly everyone else seemed surprised. People were bewildered, distraught, angry and bitter. The timing, I'm sure, had something to do with their reactions. We were acquired several weeks before Thanksgiving. But I was blown away that so many people reacted as though they did not have a clue. I heard the music, why didn't they?

Why is it that we so often don't hear the music? Or, maybe the question should be, why don't we react when we hear the music?

The music we hear can be our hearts, our mind or our subconscious saying, "Don't do it" or "Move on" or "You've had enough" or "You're going to get hurt." Your music can be your wife saying, "You don't listen to me," "You don't give me any affection anymore," "We don't do the things we used to do," and ultimately "You don't love me anymore." Your music could be your boss saying, "We're going to give the special project to someone else; hang in there, and we'll be looking at you the next time." Your music could be the silent treatment you now receive from the person who used to shower you with love letters, sweet conversation, lengthy phone calls, timely e-mails and cards of endearment. Your music could be your body grumbling that it's time for a check-up. Your music could be the vibes you intuitively feel right before you get the phone call from the friend you haven't spoken to in years.

Some people call it vibes, their gut or their intuition. I call it music.

My father did not listen to the music before we moved away. My friend Leah did not listen to the music when her husband sent her all kinds of lyrics of frustration, indicating he was ready to end their relationship. The music began to hurt her ears though, when, out of the blue, he called to say he wasn't coming back home and that there was nothing she could say or do to change his mind.

At times, when we hear the music, we ignore it, avoid it or turn it down. However, when we enjoy the beat, we turn the music up. We blast it.

You see it when sports teams and athletes make incredible comebacks after seemingly being down and out. You see it when people make monumental shifts to right their lives, professional or personal. You see it when singers and speakers get on a roll in front of audiences. They start singing songs and sharing anecdotes that weren't in the practice routine.

Sonny Elia taught and coached in the Philadelphia school system for 24 years. He became one of my Titans/Dads when I was in the ninth grade. He coached my junior varsity baseball and basketball teams. During the summer months, I went to his Mr. Basketball Camp first as a camper, then as a counselor. Today the camp is the official Philadelphia 76ers basketball camp.

Sonny's music started when teaching stopped being fun, when what once had been a passion evolved into a frustrating job. The music also took the form of more hardened, aggressive and less educationally ambitious students. The students and the resulting relationships, he insists, are what had kept him there for so long.

For a number of years he wore both hats: teacher/coach and basketball camp owner. He was unbelievably stretched. Coincidentally, when the teaching started to sour, the basketball camp business started to sweeten. Sonny had always enjoyed the business end but, up to that point, he had not listened deeply to the summer camp melodies. The music finally became its loudest when Sonny had to turn away potential campers because he did not have the facilities to accommodate his growing clientele.

He knew he needed to manage the business full time to build the basketball haven he and so many of the youths craved. Sonny listened to the music, retired from teaching and started running the business full time. He has never looked back.

Starting today, when you hear the music, turn it up. Do some research. Collect some data. Discover what's playing and why it's playing. Listen for the times the music comes on and for the times it goes off. Think about where you are when you hear it. Think about how it makes you feel when you do. And don't just listen to one type of music; expand your horizon. If it's a triumphant feeling, then keep doing what you're doing. If it's a melancholy feeling, undoubtedly, it may be time for a change. But you're going to have to do something. Awesome people listen to the music and use it to their advantage. Watch them. They are always moving to the beat.

Average: Ignoring the signals that alert you that it's time for a change or making excuses for the signals, attributing them to something else.

Awesome: Listening to the music and developing an action plan that will produce sensational results. In addition, being disciplined and diligent during the changes.

EXTRA AWESOME GIFT

I find it very sad to hear about people who go all of their lives searching for the "true meaning of life" as if it is a tangible thing that is hidden in some secret, magical place. I believe that the true meaning of life is something that we must create for ourselves. Just as I choose to create an awesome rather than average life for myself, I can also create an awesome meaning for my life.

For me the meaning of my life is in being in love with life every day and keeping my eyes open to everything it has to offer. Whether it's being in love with someone or something or a special place or time, within that love I acquire the unique kind of passion required for an awesome life. This kind of passion provides me with the courage and the energy to do awesome things, to have awesome relationships and to be an awesome individual. My eyes and heart are open to experiences every day that create that feeling of love and passion. I want to be carried away by it. The most important thing I try to remember is this:

The music of life is around us every day. You can either choose to dance to it or you can lose yourself in it. Lose yourself in the music and if you do, life, your life, will be awesome!

—Lisa Dommer (Columbus, OH)

Quickly turn to your Personal Awesome Action Plan Page (p. 238) and write the five "awesome actions" you're going to take as a result of reading this chapter. When you're finished, turn back to read more about what it takes to go from average to awesome!

GIFT 24

Be Hungreee!

The excitement about business and life is the reviewing, the renewing, and the redoing. Doing the same thing repeatedly is only marking time. I desire to make a mark, an undeniable mark and leave something behind to be fondly remembered.

—Ron Mitchell (Philadelphia, PA)

When was the last time you wanted something so desperately you could taste it? That coat, dress, suit, pair of shoes, high definition TV set, stereo, car, cruise, or ticket had your name written all over it. You could smell it, hear it, feel it, see it and would do anything imaginable to get it. You probably visited it in the store window, maybe even took some friends to see it to get their opinion. Whatever hurdles or sacrifices you were going to have to go through—getting up early, going to bed late, saving, working overtime or creative money management—you were going to do what you felt you had to do. Your life, in your opinion, would not be complete without it. You were on a mission. You were hungry, at least for a minute. Let me explain.

I've witnessed this phenomenon time and time again. I've seen well-intentioned people, not deterred by anything else going on in their lives, getting a short-lived adrenalin rush because of the importance they give a particular event, item or occasion. I've watched relentless Christmas and Easter patrons shop until they dropped before the big day. I've seen people, after long, grueling, challenging work-days, come home and thoroughly clean their house then cook all night preparing for huge family Thanksgiving dinners. I've seen sports and concert fans spend the night outside, sleeping on the ground, bundled up in blankets in freezing, winter temperatures just to purchase tickets to an event. Somehow, some way, we consistently make time, muster up the strength and put in the effort for EVENTS, but not for our DREAMS.

But what's more sustaining, events or dreams? If you said dreams, then we're on the same page. To pursue your dreams you need a special appetite. You have to be **hungreee!**

Colonel Sanders, Mr. KFC himself, was **hungreee** when he wanted to get his tasty chicken recipe on the market. Stories report that at the age of 60-something, he traveled around the world, living in his car, pitching his now famous chicken recipe. Before receiving his first contract, he supposedly had knocked on over 1000 doors.

Even Abraham Lincoln endured numerous setbacks. Research suggests that Honest Abe, in several losing elections, received less support than a Vanilla Ice, Fat Boys and Milli Vanilli reunion tour. Multitudes of successful people paid their dues many times over before finally arriving on the world's center stage. Perseverance became their breakfast, dedication their lunch and resiliency their dinner and dessert. They were **hungreee**.

Being **hungreee,** on the surface, seems like it could be one of the world's easiest assignments: identify something you want and stead-fastly pursue it with tenacity and vigor. It's this tenacity and vigor, however, that separate the *snacker* from the **hungreee**. Being **hungreee** requires a phenomenal amount of discipline, drive, determination, self-esteem and confidence. The hunger that is required to reach the perceived unreachable or obtain the so-called unobtainable is not sold on shelves or on infomercials. You can't borrow it from a friend or order it online. It comes from within you. And, trust me when I say, "IT'S NOT EASY!"

Discipline and hunger require doing something you should do when at times you don't want to. You see it in boxers, namely the contenders, who move away from their families, sentence their bodies to years of grueling, sweaty gym wars and marathon morning runs, preparing for those championship matches. You see it in teachers. They spend their lives, earning a modest income, sometimes in disadvantaged surroundings, trying to help us shape ours. You see it in social activists and protestors. In the name of justice and equality they risk it all for causes they deem significant. They've faced fire hoses, arrests, police dogs, taunts and guns while demonstrating for voting rights, education, bus riding privileges, employment and the like.

My hunger pangs started early. I started with sports, then eventually landed on more significant tasks like helping people fulfill their dreams and reach their potential.

While we were growing up, my friends and I woke up **hungreee** and went to bed **hungreee.** We would shovel the snow off of the schoolyard court to play basketball during the winter months. Sometimes we played basketball in the rain. If we didn't have a real football we used a tennis ball or rolled up pieces of aluminum foil to play two-hand touch. Sometimes we played tackle football in the snow. Our catcher and strike zone was sometimes a chalk-drawn square on the schoolyard brick wall. Sometimes we played baseball at night under the dim and flickering corner streetlights. Our relay races were around-the-block sprints; the two teams simultaneously circled the block in opposite directions as the pavement, street, parked cars, stores and houses served as our track, field and stadium. We also learned about hunger from the neighborhood bully, who always sought a rematch if any of us was fortunate enough to get the best of him in a fight.

My hunger was also evidenced in my pushing myself to uncanny limits. I would try to eclipse my "personal best" time each time I shoveled the snow and raked the leaves. I occasionally rode my bike with my eyes closed and without holding onto the handlebars. I wanted to see how far and how long I could ride without crashing. I used to see how long I could hold my breath under water when I went swimming. I would pinch my nose shut, close my eyes, and then sink to the bottom of the pool. After about 90 seconds I would lunge forward, frantically searching for air. That thrust to get air is the hunger that's needed when you're pursuing your dreams. That was how I lived then and how I now live.

Many of us fake hunger. The pangs are there, but our behavior is not in alignment with our thoughts. We say that we want something badly enough, but our actions masquerade as moments, not momentum. Think about it: we don't get in life what we want, we get what we are. That's why when life starts weeding out the pretenders from the contenders so many of us succumb. Just to see how serious and hungry you are, life will humble you. Pain and self-doubt will stare at you in the mirror each morning.

My Titan Susie Fields says she's unstoppable in her actions to support her family's and friends' goals. "To me NO means it's ON. If someone tells me NO, I find another way. I keep on keeping on. I know it sounds corny, but half of success is just getting up off your heinie one more time and trying again. How many times can you quit when success is right around the corner?"

You have to be **hungreee** if you want to restore relationships too. If I hadn't been on the "I'm mad at my dad" diet for so long, I believe our relationship could have been saved before he passed away. Many will say they're hungry, that they want to make peace, but they wait around for the other person to initiate things. Life is not a board game. It's not about spinning the needle or rolling the dice. It's something you cannot take for granted.

Since the great majority of us are visual learners, let me give you a few more pictures of what situational hunger looks like. The challenge is making it typical, not-just-in-the-moment, behavior. Create these pictures in your mind's eye. Have you ever seen someone running through the airport to make his/her flight? That's situational **hungreee**! Have you ever seen a football player relentlessly running downfield to make a tackle? That's situational **hungreee!** Have you ever seen shoppers lined up to enter a popular department store that's having a huge going-out-of-business sale? That's situational **hungreee!** Have you seen the reality show contestants (*Fear Factor*, *The Apprentice*, *Survivor* and the rest) going for the money and prizes? That's situational **hungree!** (I think some of you may believe it's insanity) I'm sure you've seen the movie depiction of two lovers running into each other's arms after a long separation. That's situational **hungreee!** Imagine if people consistently went after their dreams this way.

That's the way we have to pursue our goals, our relationships and our passions. Anything short of that is pretending.

Once you are totally committed to this new, improved way of eating–I mean living–consider this seven step process for **hungreee** management:

Step One: Be creative.

Step Two: Be intentional.

Step Three: Be focused.

Step Four: Be courageous.

Step Five: Be tenacious.

Step Six: Be consistent.

Step Seven: Be resilient.

Average: Inconsistently going after your dreams and goals. Settling for and complaining about your current reality.

Awesome: Developing an insatiable and unrelenting drive to reach your goals and fulfill your passions. Developing a hungreee attitude for winning, laughing, dreaming, loving and growing.

EXTRA AWESOME GIFTS

One of my favorite quotes is Emma Goldman's, "If I can't dance, I don't want to be part of your revolution." I love the spirit of joy amidst struggle that it captures. It has energy that lifts me up.

As an educator and activist, I draw on the courageous spirit of those who risked so much for human rights and social justice. I think of Nelson Mandela, Sojourner Truth, Frederick Douglas, Martin Luther King, Jr., Anne Braden, Cesar Chavez, Lillian Smith, Harriet Tubman, Gandhi, Malcolm X, and all the other heroes and sheroes around the globe who worked for peace, despite the dangers they faced.

Their spirit of resistance and their love for all humanity carries me on the days when I feel like change will never come. They never gave up, and we owe it to them to continue the struggle in any way we can. Helping to create a world of love, peace and equity for all people (where we can all be free to dance to whatever music we choose) is the most awesome thing I can think of!

—Patti DeRosa (Randolph, MA)

I believe that life has a turning point—a point at which we either grasp our opportunity to experience awesome or we let it slip away. My opportunity came on the morning of December 19, 1990 at a meeting of the American Society for Industrial Security (ASIS). As a young, single man, and unconnected middle manager in the security industry, I attended that local meeting looking to build my professional network, and in turn, my career. A respected leader in the group asked for volunteers to help him write and produce a monthly newsletter.

I felt like a kid in high school as I looked around the room and watched 50 or so more experienced members stare at their breakfast plates, the floor, their fingernails; they looked at everything rather than make eye contact with the meeting leader. Suddenly I received a kick from under the table from a friend, urging me to raise my hand and volunteer. To this day, I can't understand why he didn't raise his hand instead, but I thank him for his hesitation.

Several months as a writer for the newsletter led to two years as the editor, then to a year each as vice president and president of the local chapter. I was asked to expand my role as a volunteer leader regionally and then internationally as a member of the Society's Board of Directors. In 2002, I had the honor of being installed as the president of ASIS in my home city of Philadelphia—in front of my family, friends, and 18,000 of the Society's 32,000 members.

There's no denying that these accomplishments alone would make anyone feel awesome. But to me, each step has brought treasures and memories to a life that has far overshadowed the titles that I've held. I've made lifelong friends and I met my wife, Lori.

To me, awesome has no laurels to rest upon. It is an ongoing state, achieved by continuously seeking out new challenges—living each day with a purpose!

—Dan Kropp, CPP (Collegeville, PA)

Quickly turn to your Personal Awesome Action Plan Page (p. 239) and write the five "awesome actions" you're going to take as a result of reading this chapter. When you're finished, turn back to read more about what it takes to go from average to awesome!

25

GIFT

Keep Your Glasses Clean

My perspective has changed from being an unwilling receptor of change (a victim) to being a positive participant with the power to make decisions, especially about my attitude, and to contribute where my skills are needed. I've learned that I can bring light or darkness into every situation.

—Bonnie Strand (Bloomington, MN)

I remember my first day as a Widener University freshman. Deciding what to wear took the better part of my morning rush hour. Since I was now a college student, I wanted to look like one. As I rode the 309 bus to the beautiful, Chester, Pennsylvania campus, I reminisced about my high school years and pondered my upcoming college years. My immediate past had been spectacular, but my immediate future was a plot waiting to unfold.

My slate was now clean. Only the Widener football coaches and a few faculty members in the financial aid and registration offices had any idea of who James Smith was. To the remainder of the faculty and student body, I was another spry freshman taking summer classes to help better prepare for the college curriculum. C. Alan Rowe, Widener's legendary basketball coach, was my math professor. I was new and I was uncharacteristically nervous.

With my self-esteem suddenly deciding to wait for me outside the building, I walked into the classroom. Upon entering the room, I peered around and was overwhelmed with an unexpected urge to make a speedy U turn and head back home. "Do I belong here?" I thought. The room was filled with spirited, attractive, confident, 1590-on-their-S.A.T.-looking coeds. Their colorful book bags appeared new. I was still carrying the same worn, over-the-shoulder bag I had carried during my last two years of high school. Even their pencils seemed to have sharper points. They had calculators. I had a ruler and a pencil sharpener.

I reached down, picked up my envious, nervous, demotivated spirit and carried it to the back of the room. I sat down. My only words during the entire two-hour period were "I'm here," in response to hearing my name during the attendance roll call. This was certainly not like me. I always sat in the front of every room with the other over-achievers. I always walked with my head up and with a wide, assured smile and with an extra sense of urgency. You always felt my presence. Not this time, however. I let my smudged glasses get the best of me.

Smudged glasses?

Sometimes we wear our eyeglasses for days without cleaning the lenses. For some unknown reason, we don't immediately notice the spots, streaks or fingerprints. We move through life as if we see the world perfectly, clearly. Then one day we have a stroke of genius… an epiphany. Something moves us to find a Kleenex, paper towel, napkin, scarf, shirt or tie to clean our lenses and voila! The world becomes a brighter place. Ironically, up to that point, we would have vehemently argued that we could see everything just fine. But what are we missing?

Let's examine this for a moment.

Some of the dirt taking temporary residence on our lens comes from the atmosphere: rain, smog, pollution, dust particles and the like. The other smudges are "our stuff," our fingerprints. Just as the literal smudges on eyeglasses affect how we see things, the figurative smudges on our "glasses of life" affect how we move through this world, how we live our lives, how we see ourselves, how we perceive and respond to challenges and opportunities. Or as Alfred, Lord Tennyson once said, "I am a part of all that I have met."

The "stuff" we have no control over (i.e., Mother Nature and Uncle Universe) is parallel to the people and unforeseen circumstances and the like that we encounter. The "stuff" we do have control over are our emotions, reactions, perceptions, behaviors, attitudes and thoughts. Many will go to their graves arguing that they see things exactly the way they are. But that's comparable to walking around with dirty glasses.

When our glasses are dirty, very seldom do our friends, relatives and colleagues come up to us and say, "Hey, your glasses are filthy… you need to clean them." We eventually come to that realization on our own. I had no idea how dirty my glasses were when I stepped onto Widener's gorgeous campus that day. My lenses were filled with smudges of doubt, anxiety and ambivalence, mostly attributed to my minority freshman student status.

Sometimes when we take off our glasses our blind spots remain. On those occasions we should consider being open to feedback and hearing other points of view. I wrote about this in the Introduction to this book when I shared that some of my realities and perceptions may stretch some of your beliefs and perspectives.

How else can dirty glasses impact us?

The *Primetime* television show with Diane Sawyer and Chris Wallace has over the years featured episodes in which professional testers are placed in everyday America. Whether they are trying to find employment and housing, getting a tee time, buying automobiles and other merchandise, getting into their locked car, catching a taxi cab or teaching a class of first graders, the inconsistent treatment the testers received based on their age, appearance, gender, physical ability and race was startling. Even more amazing were the comments of those who provided the inconsistent treatment. To a person, despite the mountains of video evidence and footage that showed otherwise, they said that they treated all of the testers the same and that their behaviors and decisions were fair. Many, however, declined to be interviewed.

Dirty glasses help shape attitudes, biases, beliefs and a litany of "isms" and provide many of the high, moving hurdles one has to clear in order to be awesome. Dirty glasses create self-limiting beliefs and low self-esteem. Dirty glasses can end relationships. Dirty glasses can cause people to always play the blame game, never taking responsibility for their "stuff." Dirty glasses can be detrimental to your health and well-being. Dirty glasses cause insecurity.

Dirty glasses can deflate our "dream" balloons. Consider the decisions we make about employment, family, education, fitness, nutrition and relationships. Are those decisions grounded in truth and facts? Have we collected all the data? Have we taken full responsibility and accountability? Have we thoroughly researched all of our options? Or do we need to wipe off our lenses?

How many times do we talk ourselves out of opportunities? How many times do we look in the mirror and say, "Self, don't worry about it, it wasn't meant to be…you really didn't miss anything…they weren't going to give it to you anyway…they don't even like you."

One of the reasons I love what I do professionally is that I view motivational speaking, coaching, training and consulting as jobs in the glass-cleaning business.

My good friend Savannah had worked in corporate America for nearly 30 years. Having worked for two major companies during that time, she had accumulated a wealth of knowledge, expertise and positive professional relationships. She managed departments and excelled in individual contributor roles. Respected by her peers and other professional colleagues, she was a mainstay at her organizations.

However, her deep-seated drive to start her own company sang in her subconscious like a popular televison commercial jingle. The jingle never went away. Neither would the smudges on her glasses that said, "Stay here…it's safe…why give up all of these benefits…you could never make it on your own…why start all over again…most people who go out on their own never make it."

After a few more years on the job and a few more lengthy conversations with her biggest antagonist and her biggest protagonist (herself), Savannah cleaned her glasses of the fear and self-doubt. She took the plunge, leaving her safe, high-salaried Fortune 100 job and started her own company. Our last phone conversation lasted less than 30 seconds. She was too busy with client requests and projects. She had to call me back later.

I wonder what was on the lenses of:

- The players of the United States 1980 gold-medal winning Olympic hockey team before they beat the invincible Russian team in the semifinal game;

- Rosa Parks when she refused to give up her seat on the bus;

- Marian Wright Edelman when she became the first black woman admitted to the Mississippi Bar and founded the Children's Defense Fund and Stand for Children;

- John F. Kennedy when he envisioned us walking on the moon;

- David Ho when he was one of a small group of scientists who recognized AIDS as an infectious disease, and set out to discover a cure;

- Jonas Salk when he developed the Salk vaccine for polio;

- Jane Elliott when she first facilitated her "brown eyes/blue eyes" exercise in 1968 on her third graders in Riceville, Iowa to teach them a lesson in discrimination;

- Muhammad Ali when he had to choose between going to prison and fighting in the Vietnam War;

- Lance Armstrong before he mounted his bike for the first time after recovering from cancer;

- Jose Rizal when he, through the use of his powerful pen, rallied Phillipinos to believe in themselves;

- Helen Keller while she spent the most of her life advocating for poor people, women's rights, pacifism and the rights of people with disabilities;

- Steveland Morris (Stevie Wonder), when as a youngster he decided that he wanted to make sensational music by singing and playing the harmonica and piano.

Average: Thinking that you see the world perfectly, clearly...that your perceptions and thoughts are unequivocally right.

Awesome: Reexamining how you see the world and how you see yourself. Reinventing yourself. Looking for feedback and information that challenges your critical assumptions and beliefs.

Take off your glasses right now! Take a look at the lenses. How clean are they? What areas need additional cleaning? What areas get smudged the most? What are your blind spots? It's time for a major breakthrough! It's time for you to reinvent yourself! It's time for you to see more clearly! Awesome people have awesome vision!

EXTRA AWESOME GIFT

In just seven months I would step down as manager of the Philips Lighting Application Center. As I sat reviewing the latest set of very positive workshop evaluations, I thought to myself, "How close did I come to pushing this opportunity away?" Self-employed or virtually so for most of my professional life, I had been working as a successful project manager on lighting projects in Upstate New York. I was good at it and had more work than I needed. I was content, even happy. I had four grown children, a few grandchildren with more on the way. Life was good.

One phone call would change all of that.

*The day was December 28, 1998, three months before my 50th birthday. The phone rang: "Hello, yes this is he (I listened, then laughed aloud). Who put you up to this? Is this some sort of joke?" I asked. The voice on the other end replied, "No, not at all. I represent Philips Lighting Company and we want you to consider being the next manager of the Lighting Center." "Oh yes," I replied, "and what will they put in the announcement, 'Philips hires **plodder** from Buffalo?' The last person to hold that position had a Ph.D."*

Four months to the day later, I sat in my new office in Somerset, NJ in the Lighting Center, as the new manager of Lighting Education. At age 50, I was "stepping out" when most of my peers were "stepping back."

I came to Philips to do lighting education; it seemed like a good fit. Instead, what I found surprised me beyond all telling; I found my "right" work. As a consultant I was good, maybe even very good. What I had was an average expression for my gifts and talents. As I "unpacked" my role as Lighting Application Center Manager, I discovered my gifts and talents as a trainer.

I never would have uncovered these roles as a project manager in Upstate New York. The awesome part is finding my right work and having the freedom to spend the rest of my life pursuing it with a passion!

—Paul F. Hafner (Somerset, NJ)

Quickly turn to your Personal Awesome Action Plan Page (p. 239) and write the five "awesome actions" you're going to take as a result of reading this chapter. When you're finished, turn back to read more about what it takes to go from average to awesome!

26 GIFT

Wow Yourself!

Some of the things that really perk me up are the small things like a forecast promising a string of warm, sunny days; a great meal planned for the evening; or plans to see a dear friend. It doesn't have to be a large undertaking. I find great joy in the simple things in life.

—Barbara Rivera (Johnson City, NY)

"To unwind or relax after a stressful day, I go back to being a child," my friend Kim Reynolds recently told me when I asked her what she does to feel good. "I keep a stash of finger paints, coloring books and crayons (the super big ones) and I just sit at the table and draw, color and paint. I usually play some children's music in the background. It's so simple an activity that after an hour or so I'm refreshed. I then hang up one or two of my 'masterpieces' on my refrigerator as a reminder not to get stressed again. I sometimes will also put on one of my childhood videos like Willy Wonka."

The Godfather of Soul, James Brown, wrote a song many moons ago called "I Feel Good." Not a lot of variety or diversity in the lyrics, just a succession of "I feel goods." Whenever it's played today people smile and start nodding their heads to the beat. Everyone wants to feel good.

What do you do to feel good? Let's take it to another level. What do you do to Wow yourself?

What? You don't think there's enough time in the day to make special time just for you? Consider for a moment the world we're living in. We seemingly spend more time at work chasing the next promotion than we do at home (even though the average person only gets promoted six or seven times in his or her lifetime.) In addition to the work, there can be an exorbitant amount of travel involved (either driving back and forth to work, enduring the daily public transportation grind or business travel). Consider the relocation merry-go-round one can get on, depending on his/her job. The accepted term for that is "paying your dues" or "paying the cost to be the boss."

We also have to contend with our coworkers' attitudes, egos, personalities, mood shifts, mishaps, perceptions and personal problems every day. Throw in the office mumbo jumbo, rumors, backstabbing, corporate politics, mergers, acquisitions, layoffs, forced retirements, downsizing, rightsizing, reorganizing and workplace inequities, and I say you need to find a way to escape more often.

You're probably thinking that you always take a vacation. That's not enough, considering that the average person usually only takes one vacation a year. You need to feel good more often.

My suggestion? Treat yourself right! Reward yourself. No, make that Wow yourself!

As a former fulltime professional, corporate trainer, I relish working with other trainers during train-the-trainer sessions. One of my favorite questions is, asking them what they do after their training sessions are over. They say the obvious first: collect the evaluations. What else? Clean the room. What else? Review the evaluations. What else? Begin to prepare for the next session. What else? Turn off the computer and other audiovisual equipment. What else? Rest for a moment before either heading back to the office or home. What else? At that point they are usually ready to pop me upside the head. "What else is there, Jim?" they ask. "Why not reward yourself or Wow yourself for all that you've just done?" I counter.

"Let's see, you probably spent a considerable amount of time preparing your lesson," I continue. "You arrived early to set up the room. Public speaking in itself is the number one fear for adults, and you do it for a living. You counted and distributed all of the handouts and workbooks. You checked the roster and maybe even talked to some of your participants' managers. You prepared your slides and flipcharts. You undoubtedly spent extra time in the bathroom mirror that morning getting ready. You might have stayed up late the night before to ensure that you knew your stuff. Then there was all of the practice, practice, practice you put in. In all likelihood, you had to deal with some member of the **Pain In The Neck Participant Posse**."

"In no particular order," I begin, "they are: **Prisoners** (people who don't want to be there—management made their attendance mandatory); **Vacationers** (people who are not serious about the subject matter: they just attend to get away from the office pressures, kick back, eat whatever food you provide and have fun); **Party Poopers** (people who are there to ensure that no one has a good time); and **Know-It-Alls** (people who think they know everything about everything: they would rather teach the session). Just think, I did not even mention **Late Lenny, Leave Early Lee, Sandy the Sleeper, Danny the Demolitionist, Erica the Extrovert, Cedric the Complainer, Pessimistic Peter, Damon the Debater, Diego the Day Dreamer, Brad the Big Baby, Selma the Cell Phone Queen, Penny the Palm Pilot and Pager Princess** and **Newspaper Ned.** After putting up with all of them, don't you think you deserve something special? Anything shy of a Nobel Prize is probably not enough." The participants laugh, but I'm serious.

It's a forgone conclusion that we could do a much better job of rewarding and taking care of ourselves, right? Right! We could enjoy a better diet. We could work our bodies out more and drink less. We could stop smoking. We could stop procrastinating. We could stop focusing on what we don't have rather than on what we do. We could stop putting ourselves down. We could get more rest. We could read more. We could laugh and smile more. We could stop taking every-thing so seriously. We could do more and talk less. We could stop meddling in everybody else's business. We could distance ourselves from toxic people and toxic work. We could watch less TV and listen to more music. Folks, these are the basics. What about rewarding or treating yourself to something special? Even more, what about the Wow factor? When was the last time you Wowed yourself, truly treat-ing yourself to something spectacular?

What makes the Wow meter? Depending on whom you talk to:

- A full-body, from your nose to your toes, your eyes to your thighs, massage;

- An airplane seat in first class;

- Significant time with the person/people you love the most;

- Buying those shoes, you know the ones that I'm talking about (got to have them);

- A life-changing book, CD or tape;

- Prayer and meditation;

- Breakfast, lunch and dinner in bed, with someone feeding you;

- Relaxing on the deck of an ocean-front home;

- Add your favorite here _____;

Got it? Now go get it!

I prefer the simple things, too. I enjoy cooking on the grill with a cold glass of lemonade by my side, dining anywhere near water and turning into a prune in a hot tub. I also love reading the comments participants write in my scrapbook as I fly back home after a session. The scrapbook was a gift from one of my client groups.

Why not be selfish once in a while? Hold up! Why does taking care of oneself or treating oneself to something incredibly rewarding have to be considered selfish?

I have to admit that prior to turning 40, the needle on my Wow meter rested, moved, rested, rested, moved, rested, rested, rested. As the 40th anniversary of my birth was approaching, I began having intermittent pity parties about getting "OLD."

My colleague Keith and I made a sales call to one of our major clients. The opening small talk involved conversation about getting older. I mentioned to Diane Chew, one of the two clients at the meeting, that I was about to do the big 4-0 and wasn't looking forward to it. She laughed and said, "Jim, I just had this same conversation with my sister, who recently turned 40. I told her to list 40 reasons why it feels awesome to be 40. I told her not to edit her thoughts…just to write. When she finished her list, believe or not, she was a changed person. She started feeling great about herself again and decided that her next list was going to be 40 ways to treat herself right." I took Diane's advice and the needle on my Wow meter has been moving steadily ever since.

Now, after training sessions or keynote motivational addresses I'm on a Wow mission. Sometimes when I wake up, I'm on a Wow mission. I tell my friends about going on Wow missions. Now I'm telling you!

Remember, this is a "Wow-ME" mission, not a "become totally self-absorbed with myself" trip. The big three "S's" (Self-serving, Self-centered and Selfish) have no place in this discussion. This chapter is a reminder for you to stop neglecting your happiness: to make a concerted effort for MUCH more fun, pampering and relaxation—to provide more spectacular rewards for you!

Since we've been conditioned and socialized to work until we're exhausted and to always wait for significant occasions to plan something special, we settle into a BORING, daily routine.

 We should eat the dessert first sometimes.

Don't wait for guests to come over to use your best Lennox. What occasion are you waiting for to wear that special outfit!? What are you

Average: Working hard but seldom making time to relax and reward yourself for all of your efforts and all that you endure personally and professionally.

Awesome: Treating yourself special more often. Wowing yourself with those things and those people that bring the biggest smile to your face and to your heart.

saving for now? Don't you deserve better? Don't you deserve to be treated as AWESOME more often? Then don't wait for others to do it. Once you begin Wow-ing yourself more often you'll find it easier to Wow others!

EXTRA AWESOME GIFT

How do I Wow myself? I get 100 on my spelling tests. I like buying new clothes. I like going to visit Grammy. I go to the Disney store. I like watching my favorite movies, Peter Pan, Shrek and Corrina Corrina, on DVD. I play with Max (my cat) and I like playing my piano in recitals. Going to school every day and being in Mrs. "J's" class, playing with my friends Kylie, Korel, Sabria and Heather and spending time with my mommy and daddy makes me feel Wow. I like going to Grandmom Tina's house, too. Oh, one more thing, I like seeing Princess Jasmine, The Little Mermaid and Tinker Bell at Disney World.

—Daecia Smith (written at age 7, now 9 West Berlin, NJ)

Quickly turn to your Personal Awesome Action Plan Page (p. 239) and write the five "awesome actions" you're going to take as a result of reading this chapter. When you're finished, turn back to read more about what it takes to go from average to awesome!

27

GIFT

Get the Junk Out of YOUR Trunk!

It's not the load that breaks you down—it's the way you carry it.

—Lena Horne

I woke up at 6:15 AM with my office on my mind. The kind of work I was about to dive into was not the usual, however. No reading files. No checking voicemail. No computer work. I, with energy in my step and creativity in my head, was on a Feng Shui mission.

I started by throwing out the old magazines. Outdated issues of *PC, Forbes* and *New Jersey* bit the dust first. Next went the old shoes, shoe polish, sneakers and everything else on my closet floor. All of those items were getting a one-way ticket to Goodwill. My ancient, typewritten company manuals and facilitator's guides, which I had not referenced in what seemed like 300 years, were next. I privately escorted them to my garage.

The old file folders also received their walking papers. "Old this," "forgotten that," and "haven't used this in a long time," were all moved out of my home office.

I lit several candles. Opened my curtains. The sun said, "Whas-suuupppp?!?!?!?" I rearranged pictures and other important files and could now actually see the plush gray carpet that I've walked on nearly every day for the past seven years, but never really appreciated. I cleared my desk—wow, the calendar was actually still there. No, I was not auditioning for an appearance on a cable fix-up-your-house show, nor was I participating in some kind of cleaning marathon. My mission: to continue unloading the junk (figurative and literal) from my trunk.

The day before my office rampage, I spent the afternoon receiving coaching and book-publishing direction from my Titan, colleague and friend, Leslie Shields. Leslie and her sister Cydney authored the book *Work Sister Work* in 1993. Upon entering Leslie's home, I immediately found myself in a mental place of relaxation, serenity and calm. Every piece of furniture rested in the perfect spot. Imaginary "children under 21 not allowed" signs hung from the walls. Not only could you eat off the floor, you could probably also eat off the welcome mat and backyard ground.

The living room, where the meeting took place, was AWESOME! The rich, cobalt-blue painted walls, which were not blocked by a bevy of art and other pictures, were empowering and energizing. A Snickers Bar brown wall unit filled with African American dolls and figurines captured my attention every time my mind drifted from the meeting. Finishing touches included a bronze love seat, cream sofa, brown bureau with computer and printer hidden inside and loving family photos on top, television, stereo unit and a selection of CDs that reminded me why I'm still in love with the music of the 70s and 80s.

Throw in the sweet fragrance from the candles and the sunlight that attended the meeting, and you had tranquility, a room that whispered to guests to take off your shoes and chill out. This room commandeered all of your stresses, anxieties and worries.

When I asked Leslie about the room she said it was her sanctuary, another indication for how she lives her life. "I keep it simple, Jim," she said. "I don't crowd my life or my personal surroundings with too much stuff. It can become overwhelming. Too much to fix...too much to think about...too much to clean. I just keep things basic and simple. My family members are always asking me when I'm going to put paintings on the wall. I ask them why should I cover up these beautiful blue walls? Serenity and simplicity work best for me."

I drove home that evening listening to a CD of Jermaine Jackson's greatest hits and thinking about the incredibly inspiring meeting we had just completed. I spent time prioritizing the 29 items that Leslie and I created for my *From Average to Awesome* to-do list. I also thought about the energy and calm that I felt while in Leslie's home.

My immediate plans were simple—to work toward making my office, my surroundings, my work and my life simpler. Get the junk out of my trunk. There were too many old magazines, manuals and files in my office taking up the space and room that new books and resources could occupy. All of the unused materials selfishly created a workspace of clutter, not creativity.

Junk is anything that prevents you from being awesome. Your trunk is your life.

Literally and figuratively, there are unnecessary things, things we seldom use, which we drive around with for years. The items, from time to time, roll around in the trunk making enough noise to remind us they're still there. The junk is weighty enough to slow our drive as we head up steep hills. In addition, the junk takes up much-needed space. Given those facts, one would reason that we would remove all of the junk out of our trunk—and fast.

Instead, we take it with us everywhere, moving other items around to make room for it, eventually storing new "stuff" in the back seat. You need proof? The next time you leave the grocery store after an hour of food shopping, and you pull your shopping cart full of groceries up to your trunk for loading, you will know what I'm talking about.

Metaphorically, the junk in one's life trunk can be like kryptonite. Kryptonite? Remember the powerful superhero Superman? Despite the bulging muscles that stretched his tight, blue superhero uniform to the bursting point, Superman had a weakness: Kryptonite! He did his utmost to avoid that green substance that rendered him helpless and powerless. And if not for Lex Luther and the other villains who indefatigably attempted to curtail the man of steel's crime-fighting career, Superman would never have come into contact with it.

The difference between Superman and us was that the man with the muscles avoided kryptonite, his junk. We hold on to ours for dear life. We work for ours. We cell phone ours every day. We page ours. We date ours. We check in with ours about important life decisions. We spend Saturday afternoons polishing and buffing ours. We log on to ours. We eat and drink ours and buy more when we run out. We look for kryptonite qualities in the people we date. Sometimes we ask others if we could borrow some of their kryptonite. Some of us never leave home without it. Kryptonite is deadly junk! It kills our drive and our spirit. We have to get it out of our trunk.

Bronwen, a close friend, recently told me about how her friend, Denny, summoned the courage to get rid of his kryptonite. She said that his sales job caused him severe pain! As a result he was going through life rather than growing through life every day. On the surface the job seemed okay, but it was toxic. It was killing him! Kryptonite 100-Denny 2.

People saw him as a hard-working, corporate professional. He made good money, had super benefits. Denny definitely needed the bennies; he was married with two young children. Relatively speaking, on the outside he appeared to be very successful. On the inside, his spirit was eroding. The inner conflict (he hated what he was doing, he wasn't being creative, and the job was crushingly routine) was taking its toll. Have you ever had a job that you disliked so much you dreaded driving anywhere near it on your days off? That was Denny.

Sleepless nights, mood shifts and inertia were as common to him as jewelry is to QVC and Mr. T. One day he came home, sat down at the kitchen table and began to cry—one of those heaving, sniffling, heart-breaking, can't-catch-your-breath sobs. His wife, Judy, took a front row seat. Trying to compose himself, Denny said, "I'm spiritually and emotionally dead...I hate my job." "Well, what do you want to do?"

Judy asked. "I want to create beautiful furniture and art objects for people...to create a beautiful home for someone," he replied. Judy, to her credit, did not go rapid fire into the myriad family responsibilities and obligations they shared. She simply said, "Well, then, that's what we're going to do."

Shortly after his kryptonite meltdown Denny quit his job and started his own business. Those were some lean years, he had told Bronwen: "Sometimes we couldn't put a meal together and we had to accept help from Judy's parents from time to time; that really bothered me." Gradually, Denny's clients began to spread the word about the generous, warm man who designed incredibly beautiful furniture and art objects. As his confidence grew, his apparent love for his work became an uplifting statement to those who met him.

Soon Denny advertised in the *Wall Street Journal.* He has since done work for Bill Cosby, Carolyn Roehm, the Smithsonian Institute and former Secretary of State George Schultz. Not only does he create beautiful objects for his clients, but he also imparts his effusive joy for living. He got rid of the kryptonite that was in his trunk.

Let's keep it real. Kryptonite and other junk is not going to go away merely because you say, "Kryptonite, junk, it's time for you to get your hat and coat and leave." This stuff is powerful. If you don't get rid of your kryptonite, it will get rid of you!

Junk can also take the shape of a long-time friend whom you allow to soak up too much of your precious time with the same draining, depressing sob stories. Every time you see her you cringe, thinking about enduring her upcoming soliloquy. She may even become irritated because you appear happy. "Why are you so happy?" she will ask.

The junk in your trunk can also be the television set that you turn on as soon as you wake up in the morning or when you return home after work or that you watch well into the night and early morning. Junk can watch you as you watch it (see computer and video games like Hearts, Solitaire, Free Cell, Play Station and Madden 2005).

Junk can be the barrels of "other people's stuff" that you carry with you each day. You go to work thinking about their problems. You think about their problems during the workday. And you think about their problems as you drive home from work. That's what you call going to work before you get to work, working, then working over-time as you go home. We get so absorbed in everyone else's front lawn that we find little time to pull out our own weeds.

What's more, we overuse the proverbial excuse, "Well, he needs me...he would do it for me." It's just that you never give him an opportunity to help you because you're always helping him. Certainly, there's nothing wrong with lending a helping hand or ear. Some people, however, attempt to use their "help credit card" when they know the available balance is in the negative.

Once you begin your unloading you certainly could benefit by having an awesome supporting cast (see Judy, Denny's wife). The first step, though, is assertively declaring that you're going to rid yourself of that power-draining source...then do it! Other tools for this arduous job include prayer, commitment, discipline, stick-to-itiveness, cour-age and desire. If your junk is a person, you will have to change the script and rewrite the role that person plays in your life. If your junk is an object, ask yourself, until you're blue in the face, does my junk move me closer to or further away from the person I want to be?

You're going to need a new routine and a new reward system, because there's retention in repetition. And you're probably, unfortu-nately, going to have to experience an enormous amount of pain. I've come to realize that many of us don't make changes until it REALLY, REALLY hurts.

If we are going to go on this journey from average to awesome, we have to ask ourselves how we can make our travels swift and less cumbersome if we're carrying around junk. And when we do have to scale that steep hill called drama, the junk will undoubtedly keep us there a lot longer than if our trunks were empty.

An additional point to consider: sometimes the junk in our car is so quiet we forget that it's there. Remember, kryptonite radiates. Just bring your car, your life to a sudden, immediate, abrupt stop and your kryptonite, will roll to the front. What a reminder!

So, are you ready for awesome? Additional breakthrough tips for your journey are in the next chapter. Please do not begin reading this chapter until you've started to remove the junk from your trunk. You would not want anything to slow you down now, would you? Here's a cheat sheet for getting the junk out of your trunk: discard it, unload it, rewrite the role it plays in your life, avoid it and forget its phone number. Remember, you are not powerful when you are around it. Just remember Superman.

Average: Moving through life carrying the weight of other people's problems and your life's hiccups into your every day.

Awesome: Proactively addressing the aspects of your life that make you sluggish—those things that slow you from being your awesome self. Eliminating the bad habits, time drainers and toxic people that make noise in your life, like junk in your trunk.

EXTRA AWESOME GIFT

My Feng Shui consultant and career coach put the keys in the trunk and turned. The trunk popped open and staring at me was years of junk—and a business relationship that was killing me. Before I hired Tamra, I was not able to bring myself to look at what was obvious to all those around me. Ever since, however, things have been wonderful.

Before my relationship with Tamra, I sold a pregnancy product, for about eight years, to insurance companies and women's health centers. During the later part of this time a struggle developed between the product's publisher and me. I, in major denial, viewed the struggle as just a bump in the road. I kept telling myself that things would eventually improve when sales and other business initiatives righted themselves. I just had to keep my focus on the vision.

Our struggle continued. Our view of what needed to happen for the product continued to differ. Our relationship was really strained. Things began to get funky financially too. My growth within my company came to a standstill. My focus on the vision became fuzzy, but I kept plodding along. I believed that we had worked too long together to bring things to an end. Besides, this was the longest business or personal relationship I had ever had so I wanted to make sure that I was doing everything to make things work.

Then Tamra came into my life. She immediately realized that there was something in my life that was causing a great deal of pain and sapping my energy. She asked me, "When will you be done with this relationship?" I said, "In three months time," even though up until she had asked the question I didn't even know an end was in sight. Coincidentally, during this same time, the publisher said that she would be going in a new direction and that she believed our business arrangement should come to an end. I agreed wholeheartedly. Rather than trying to convince the publisher that I should be a part of the new direction, that we could make a new commitment to each other, I let go. When I let go I allowed space for something more spectacular to come into my life. Knowing my history up to that point, though, if it weren't for Tamra, I probably would have fought to keep my old, stressful arrangement. I needed help and I got it.

—Bettina Carey (Seattle, WA)

Quickly turn to your Personal Awesome Action Plan Page (p. 239) and write the five "awesome actions" you're going to take as a result of reading this chapter. When you're finished, turn back to read more about what it takes to go from average to awesome!

28
GIFT

Enjoy Your Awesome Journey!

As a firm believer in the "oneness" of humankind and the fact that we're all on many individual journeys, I selfishly recognize that making the world better for others is in fact making the world better for myself, as well as paving a smoother path for my next journey.

—*Barry Callender (Nashville, TN)*

I'm not average and neither are you. I want to be happy and so do you. I desire the best for everyone that I come to know and this book is one giant thank-you card. I thank you for the cheers and for the jeers, but most importantly, I thank you for the lessons—your gifts.

I really got to know myself during the initial writing then revising of *From Average to Awesome*. Replaying the memories and experiences that shaped who I am was both painful and centering. Talking to others in the midst of their awesome journey was also both trying and revealing. And attempting to craft a book that shared my hurdles and hurrahs on the road to awesome in a way that didn't make me come across as trite, commercial, pompous or angry was probably the most challenging task.

Writing might have been easier if I had disappeared from the workplace or had gone into seclusion. I could have taken an extended vacation somewhere in the mountains and just written. I could have stopped taking calls and shut down my business operations for some time. But I made the conscious decision to live my life and run my business as usual, but with just a lot more late-night and early-morning typing, both in hotels and at home. I chose this path because I did not want to put my journey to awesome on pause and I wanted to continue to collect insights, anecdotes and gifts for the book.

I mentioned during the book's Introduction that my goal was to share anecdotally and through my Titans, colleagues and friends how I've moved from average to awesome. To make this happen, I said I would share a number of hurdles I've had to clear to get there. One of those hurdles, and perhaps the most difficult to discuss, was race. Actually, during my first few drafts, I barely mentioned race. I felt that was the safe way out—it wouldn't cause anyone to close the book in disgust—but it did not totally reflect my story.

Through this dilemma I learned:

 Not to sensor my spirit, my words and my thoughts.

Patti DeRosa, my friend and diversity mentor, after reading an early draft of my manuscript, told me to stop talking in code. She said to be clear, concise and to say exactly what I meant. I knew, after that feedback, that I had to write to express, not to impress. I had to write to disclose and not to baby-sit other's reactions to my realities.

I couldn't leave it up to the reader to read between the lines to uncover my truths. As I revisited the text, I began to wonder how often I had talked in code during my corporate days.

I then sensed that some of the experiences I would share would surprise some of my colleagues and upset others. I've always been, in the eyes of my peers and colleagues, hard-working, driven, committed and amiable Jim Smith, Jr. Many of my white friends never heard me discuss issues of race and how I thought the unfair treatment I received at times was more than just corporate politics and miscalculated judgment. Nor did I ever share that playing Jackie Robinson got tiresome sometimes, and that I missed not seeing and working with more black corporate leaders and professionals. I toiled in corporate America for a number of years and during that time I grew and matured into the person I am today. Yes, race was *one* of my major hurdles to awesome but there *were others*, many others. I was challenged with sharing this message without sounding like "the angry black man." Helping people to appreciate and understand your plight (e.g., class, education, family, gender, parenting, race and education) especially when theirs is so different is a daunting task. Nevertheless, it's my story and I'm sticking to it.

 With any journey, you need to take fuel along.

My fuel was my beliefs, together with my family and friends who supported me during my moody, unproductive, idea-less, fatigued moments, and my numerous colleagues who helped with editing, ideas, encouragement and support. As I continue on this awesome journey, I will never forget to pack their pictures and words in my suitcase and in my heart. Waking up in the middle of the night in some hotel room, in some city, will never be the same. I will awaken to pictures of my Titans on my nightstand.

Frank Sinatra sang, "Regrets, I've had a few, but then again too few to mention." I guess that about sums up my professional journey and maybe yours, too. I worked for three industry leaders and learned plenty about myself professionally and personally. I also learned that I can be awesome no matter what! And that's what I want you to take with you! Say goodbye forever to the excuses. Know that "but" is an argument for our limitations and when we argue for our limitations we get to keep them. You have to get out of your own way and hold yourself responsible for your tomorrows.

Awesome is a choice. It's about transcending barriers and being true to oneself at the same time. It's living with passion and with a purpose. It's not cursing the establishment. It's getting the establishment to see your greatness. When it comes to being awesome, good enough is not even close to being good enough. Step up! Bring it! Fire hard, kid!

I hope this book challenged you to go searching. Hey, really, I'm no one special. I'm Jim Smith, Jr., Nanci's oldest son, Rodney's brother and Daecia's dad. I don't possess any super powers and I didn't graduate from college in two months. I'm just like you. I've worked extremely hard; you've read about my blood, sweat and tears. I can't recall too many things that were just handed to me. I had to go after them. It's become part of who I am. If there's no test, then there's no testimony. If there's no mess, then there's no message. That's why I know anyone can be awesome. But you have to be open to pain and possibilities, and push back and be persistent. When in trouble I go back to my roots, my lessons, my beliefs and my Titans.

The consulting firms I've partnered with have also added to my "awesome stew." One group in particular helped me solidify in my mind that I wanted to take my professional training and speaking to a larger audience. I was one of their groupies for eight years, chasing this supreme training and consulting group from training conference to training conference, inhaling their plethora of creative training techniques, until I finally received my uniform in 1998.

During my journey I've also learned to "shake it off" and stay focused and hungreee. I've winced and then have come back. Benjamin Mays said, "It must be borne in mind that the tragedy of life does not lie in not reaching your goal—it lies in having no goal to reach." And when others demonstrated through word or deed that they were not on my team, I used their taunts like a pole-vaulter uses his or her pole to clear the bar. Les Brown says,

 "Don't get even, get ahead…let personal and professional happiness be your panacea."

When I met my photographer Pat Harmon at Barnes & Noble, I had no inclination that we were going to put the ribbon around this book writing project before I left. I was there to discuss our upcoming photo shoot.

After two hours of photo talk we moved into an update on my book. Excitedly, I explained that I was nearly finished, save a powerful close. Pat stood up and said, "Follow me." We walked over to the section where the other motivational and inspirational authors lived. There was Gotham Chopra and Iyanla Vanzant, James Redfield, Kristine Carlson and Erin Brockovich, Les Carter and Katie Couric, Gary Zukav and Richard Carlson, Pat Croce and Jim Smith, Jr. Yes, Jim Smith, Jr.! I saw *From Average to Awesome* on the Barnes & Noble shelf! I felt a rush of exhilaration! I knew that some day soon I would return and buy a copy right from this very shelf.

With my Jim Brickman CD playing in the background, I began to bring the first edition of this book to a close. My journey to awesome is ongoing. I still have a little junk in my trunk to remove and some baggage to discard. My glasses need to be cleaned every now and then and I have to monitor my "you can DO anything" zeal at times. I have to be mindful not to deposit any bad checks. And I will spend more time with my Titans and continue to make my life simpler, have more balance.

I know that there is plenty to still learn. Although I'm on an endless pursuit of awesome, I'm still going to bump my head. I'm still going to fumble the ball every now and then and I'm not always going to make the best decision. I've learned that the journey is more important than the final stop.

We pick up passengers and experiences, memories and mentors, trials and testimonials. But one thing I will do is keep exploring, keep asking questions and keep pushing myself. Isn't that what the journey is all about? I'm hungreee for knowledge. I'll continue to call on the 41 *Plus* lessons I've shared with you as well as those that I'm sure are coming my way.

I HAVE NOT DONE MY BEST WORK YET! How about you? I'm still moving from average to awesome! How about you?

Average: Taking life as it comes, from one day to the next. Being reactive rather than proactive.

Awesome: Realizing that every day is another day in your journey. Making every attempt you can to make the next day better than the one before. Learning from the insights you obtain along the way and making a difference.

EXTRA AWESOME GIFT

I am a dreamer, a true romantic. I always have been and I always will be. I count on me. No one else can bring me down. I have become an awesome person simply by dealing with each new step on my life's journey, no matter how painful or how embarrassing. I have learned from every boulder that landed in front of me. I have learned from both the things I fell victim to—and those things that were out of my control—and also by the poor decisions I've made. I believe that some of the most beautiful, honest and loving people are those who have truly LIVED and have truly LEARNED. I have! Life's journey is just that: a path given to us to walk and learn from each step of the way. It isn't meant to be straight; we'd never learn that way.

—Nancy Rebecca (Chicago, IL)

Quickly turn to your Personal Awesome Action Plan Page (p. 240) and write the five "awesome actions" you're going to take as a result of reading this chapter. When you're finished, turn back to read more about what it takes to go from average to awesome!

AWESOME REFLECTIONS PAGE...

GIFT

Understand That Awesome Challenges ALWAYS Await You

My grandmother Fannie Mae Gillis, who I rarely saw as I was growing up, had a profound affect on me. Regardless of where she was you felt her power. Everybody in my family called her Momma. She was very spiritual, intuitive and positive. I remember one particular life-changing moment we had when I was a little girl. Having noticed that I was not happy, she came up to me as I was lying in bed and said, "Gina, regardless of what happens everything is going to be all right baby; everything, is going to be all right." She said it twice. Nothing else. Her words penetrated me. I have held onto those words my entire life. No matter what trials, tribulations, valleys or heartache I've encountered, I've known that everything was going to be all right.

—*Gina M. Williams (Mt. Laurel, NJ)*

People clapped. They cried. They roared with giddy laughter. They cheered, "Go Jim. Go Jim. Go Jim. Get busy. Get busy. Get busy."

Afterwards they stood in a loooooooooong line to buy and have me autograph their copy of *From Average to Awesome*. This felt incredible. I was beaming. "I could really get used to this," I thought to myself. It had all finally come together. I did it! This two-year writing project, which took me back through my childhood and all the way up to my present, was a taxing, painful, but needed journey. There had been many memories, many warts, many tears and many gifts. But as Gloria Gaynor sang, *I Will Survive*. And I did.

My Titans, family members, colleagues and others, turned out in significant numbers. The tiny theater on Broad Street in Philadelphia, typically used for jazz shows, was bursting at the seams with over 200 people for the launch of my book. This was July 30, 2002. The book, *From Average to Awesome: 41* Plus *Gifts in 41* Plus *Years,* officially took its first step and I was well on my way to huge things… or so I thought.

I had dreamed of some semblance of a book tour with book signings and additional speaking opportunities after that night. In that dream I'd envisioned feature stories in the local Philadelphia newspapers, national magazines as well as in *USA Today*. I also hoped that a major publisher would come in and sign me to a book deal. Oprah? Of course, I was going to be on her show and in her book club.

Things didn't pan out that way, however. Instead of admirers, opportunities and success, the things that stood in line waiting to enter my life were challenges, problems, misfortune and humility. In the long run, they turned out to be more gifts, but they sure didn't feel that way at the time.

Yes, articles were written about me. Both Temple and Widener, my two colleges, kick-started things. A couple of the smaller local newspapers wrote features, too. My overtures to other magazines and newspapers didn't quite work out.

Securing a literary agent was also a "swing-and-a-miss" proposition. That's not uncommon for self-published authors, but it still didn't sit well with me. "Just meet me and read my story, you'll want to take me on as a client," I believed. This was wishful thinking.

Actually, there were some book signings. These became powerful lessons in humility, though. My brother and I set up a number of them, mostly in Philadelphia and Delaware. After the first several signings, it dawned on me that few people knew who I was. I had spent much of my adult life in corporate America and no one had heard of Jim Smith, Jr. I hadn't embezzled or laundered money from my organizations. I hadn't changed my identity. I didn't have a surreal story. I wasn't a gold medallist. I hadn't overcome a debilitating sickness. I hadn't pulled a family from a burning house. I hadn't sold 3000 books from my car trunk yet. And I didn't yet have a recognizable name in the African-American community, unlike Charles Barkley, Colin Powell and Johnnie Cochran, each of whom had a book published around the time *From Average to Awesome* came out. "Also unlike those guys," I thought in frustration, "I wrote my entire book all by myself; I didn't have a ghost writer or a co-writer." But readers generally want to read about someone they've heard about. My story, in the public's estimation, wasn't yet ready for prime time.

I remember those first signings as though they happened yesterday. I would sit either inside or outside of the bookstore at the book-signing table (with my books placed neatly and strategically by my side) watching people look at me, trying to figure out if I was somebody. My smile and encouraging wave didn't work too often. I sat there thinking that there *will* come a time in my life when these bookstores were going to be packed. Folks would be dying, I mean living, to meet me and buy my book. The ironic thing is that I would be (in my mind) the same person then as I was now. But they would view me differently. That was my motivation, my drive. Until then, at least at that point, it was another mall, another bookstore, another two to ten books sold. Thank goodness for my motivational speaking gigs and clients. That's when I sold hundreds of books. People got the opportunity to see me do my thing… and in front of their very eyes I became somebody.

Next challenge: my second marriage was falling apart. It took its toll on me. Everyone knows how trying separation and divorce can be; I don't have to belabor that point. In addition, my little pumpkin, my daughter Daecia, and I had to reinvent our relationship. Seeing her only every other weekend, and sometimes during the week when I drove from Philadelphia (I initially moved back in with my mother) to New Jersey to take her to school in the morning, was very different. I often cried when we had to say goodbye.

I remember when I knew for sure that things were not going to work out in my marriage. I drove to Daecia's school, pulled her out of class for a few minutes, and gave her non-stop hugs and kisses. She said, "Daddy you're silly." I told her that I loved her tremendously. She went back into class and I went back to trying to organize my life, which was becoming increasingly humbling. I was a forty-one year old author, international speaker, consultant and professional trainer now living with my mom. Wow—that's certainly not where I had planned to be at this point.

It got better—I mean worse. Business slowed up immensely. Opportunities were harder to find than a New Year's Eve party without resolutions, alcohol and dancing. I went into January 2003 with just one workshop on the calendar. In February there were two. Creditors began calling with a vengeance and my clients, when I did secure some work, didn't send in their checks quickly enough to help me manage my mounting debt. "I've been here before," I thought. "Why now? Why me? I just finished my book! Where's the reward for all of my hard work? This 'awesome' thing isn't easy!"

My other awesome discovery was what I learned about me. No matter what the world sends my way, I do my best to live an "awesome" life every day. Nevertheless, I was growing tired, frustrated and impatient with people who didn't seem to be trying as hard as I was, especially if I had to interact with them. Because of my business and travel activities I was running into plenty of them. Airline personnel security people, cab drivers, waiters, hotel staff and other customer-service providers were becoming daily challenges. (Of course, not all of these professionals fell into this category, but I encountered enough to last several lifetimes.) They seemed generally unhappy about what they were doing or whom they were doing it for, and it showed in the service they provided. They were grouchy, curt, disrespectful and argumentative.

I would become annoyed because I let their behavior bother me (rather than ignore it), and I was disappointed that they weren't doing something about it. I developed a bad habit of wanting to help people fix their situation when I sensed their displeasure. I was consistently losing sight of the notion that people will change when they, and only they, choose to change. I was also forgetting the fact that some people must perform jobs they didn't choose just to survive—to keep a roof over their heads and food on the table—and that I should cut them some slack. I didn't like the impatience and lack of empathy I was discovering in myself; I had to so something and do something quickly.

I reread my book.

I rededicated my life to being awesome.

I vowed to learn from my post-book experiences, realizing that those experiences have only made me stronger.

I promised myself to always be a leader, to make lemonade out of the lemons that are bound to come my way. I had to work on my mindset. That's where everything starts.

How does one do it? In addition to the other gifts I've mentioned in the previous chapters, consider these seven "second-edition, what-I've-been-reminded-of" tips:

- Shift your mindset to ward off distractions. Sometimes this means not responding to something that you know is wrong or off-base, or responding in a way that doesn't prolong the disagreement/conversation. Become mentally impenetrable.

- Become the CEO of you (i.e., take care of yourself, invest in yourself, protect yourself and take pride in yourself).

- Avoid trying to fix everyone's problems, regardless of who they are. Remember, people are not always going to do things the way you'd like them to. Their reality is different from your perception of them.

- Expect challenges, especially when you appear to be handling things in a positive way. Be proactive, not reactive.

- Keep showing up for life every day. My theory, as it relates to dealing with the world each day, is: Wake up, get up, show up, step up, then shake them up!

- Own who you are. Stop making excuses (and conjuring up reasons) for your shortcomings. Own your stuff. Confront your demons. Stop blaming others.

- Take good written and mental notes on your conversations. Always get clarity. Miscommunication causes confusion, confrontation and consternation.

"Awesome" is a way of life. You truly have to understand yourself before you can begin to understand others. This is vital since we let others impact our realities so often. You may want to consider some sort of transformation work to get to the core of what may be preventing you from being awesome. If you really want to change and improve, you have to become a life-long student.

Average: Resting on your laurels, thinking that past accomplishments will carry you for an extended period of time.

Awesome: Consistently moving forward with self-enrichment and improvement, taking ownership for all that happens to you. Learning from your highs and your lows and leveraging both for better tomorrows, realizing that things are not always going to go the way you'd like regardless of the work you put in. Also, allowing others the time and space to grow at their pace, not yours and in a direction they, not you, have chosen.

As for me, I still have a wonderful relationship with my daughter. We do "daddy-daughter" stuff all of the time. From homework and spelling tests over the telephone to taking in movies and visiting bookstores on the weekends, we are continuing to grow, not simply go, through life. Last summer we even spent eight wonderful days in Spain. One of the highlights of our trip was flying there and back first-class.

Business has picked up tremendously. This book has played a key role in creating many new opportunities. And my next two books, *Crash and Learn: Stuff Trainers Do in the Classroom That Make People Want to SHOUT, sleep or Sneak Out* and *Masters of Success*, co-authored with Ken Blanchard and other powerful speakers, are due out this year. I've continued to surround myself with incredible people, one of whom, Milt Adams (and Beaver's Pond Press), is publishing the second edition of this book.

Most importantly, I feel more awesome than ever. I welcome challenge and I welcome change. I still have more work to do—awesome people are always busy!

EXTRA AWESOME GIFT

The greatest gifts I have been given in life are my children, Aaron and Dana. When my husband and I were considering starting a family, I thought it would be as easy as making the decision to have children, getting pregnant and nine months later, adding the joy and love of a child to your life.

I came from a big family. My mom had five children. I just knew that my husband, Chris, and I would be great parents. We decided to start a family right after we were married. Within a few months I became pregnant. Yes! Everything was working according to plan and falling into place. However, just two months into my pregnancy my glee was dashed by miscarriage. This was an extremely difficult time, but everyone assured me that this was just a bump in the road to parenthood. We were told not let this dim the light of our "family" dream.

Getting pregnant a second time took what seemed like forever, but we were committed. I finally tested positive again. Days flew by as we made it past the three-month mark. We were well on our way to being parents! As my belly began to grow, we planned, decorated and created a magnificent nursery where I envisioned that we would nurture, love and care for our baby. I was six months pregnant and beaming. Everything was perfect until that snowy, Saturday in November.

Once again, we lost our baby.

This loss was heartbreaking.

We knew this baby and felt we'd created a lasting bond. I was devastated.

It wasn't until my third miscarriage that doctors had given me a less than 50% chance of ever carrying a child. At first I was crushed. I had accomplished everything else in life that I had put my mind to, but it was beginning to look like I would never have children. In time, I began to accept that realization, convincing myself that it was OK. We decided to adopt, but then I became pregnant again. The doctors were very grim, offering no more than a 20% chance of a positive outcome. We were very realistic about the potential risks and outcomes. It was an extremely long 10-month pregnancy. Finally, Aaron, our gorgeous baby boy with curly hair and deep dimples, was born.

There were several more miscarriages along the way, but three years later, my daughter, Dana, arrived. Our family was complete. It was only through the years that followed that I came to realize that the wonderment and joy of parenting is in living each moment with our family. As we enjoyed those moments, I've had the privilege of influencing and being influenced by my children and their friends. My children are grown now. Both have completed college and are on their own. We continue to share in their ups and downs, and most importantly in their love. Looking back, I knew there were many times when I thought I would never be able to ever give birth. Moreover, there have been times when I thought I was a terrible parent. My children have taught me that it's not so important that I am an awesome parent, but that we are an awesome family. We can continue to endure every challenge and make it together!

—*Marilyn Massaro (Weston, FL)*

Quickly turn to your Personal Awesome Action Plan Page (p. 240) and write the five "awesome actions" you're going to take as a result of reading this chapter. When you're finished, turn back to read more about what it takes to go from average to awesome!

THE 41 *PLUS* GIFTS

Gift 1: File, Save, Open, and Print

Gift 2: Savor Your Moments

Gift 3: Remember Your Titans

Gift 4: Get Mad, Get Sad, Get Better, Get Busy

Gift 5: Ready, Aim, Fire Up an Awesome Day!

Gift 6: Fire Hard, Kid!

Gift 7: Start Playing More Reader Rabbit!

Gift 8: Stop Depositing Bad Checks

Gift 9: Say Cheese!

Gift 10: Wear Your Own Jersey

Gift 11: Say What You Mean and Mean What You Say

Gift 12: Let Your Light Shine

Gift 13: Believe You Can Fly

Gift 14: Some People are Just Not Going to Clap

Gift 15: Be Yourself, Because Everyone Else is Taken

Gift 16: You're Not Always Going to Get the Best Hand

Gift 17: Sssssshhhh…Listen to Your Own Advice

Gift 18: Have a Forgiving Spirit

Gift 19: Remember That the Cure for the Pain is in the Pain

Gift 20: Start With the Wing First!

Gift 21: It's Not Always All About You

Gift 22: Dance Like Nobody's Watching

Gift 23: Listen to the Music

Gift 24: Be Hungreee!

Gift 25: Keep Your Glasses Clean

Gift 26: Wow Yourself!

Gift 27: Get the Junk Out of YOUR Trunk

Gift 28: Enjoy Your Awesome Journey!

Gift 29: Understand that Awesome Challenges ALWAYS Await You

Gift 30: Life without problems would be death. You know you can only have good because of evil, sweet because of sour.

Gift 31: We spend more time with our Titanics than we do with our Titans. Why?

Gift 32: Life can only be understood backwards, but it must be lived forwards.

Gift 33: Any day that you're blessed to wake up is an awesome day.

Gift 34: The quality times you spend with your loved ones are the coins that keep your life meter running.

Gift 35: Listen to both the said and the unsaid.

Gift 36: All changes begin with a change in your self-concept; you can change your outer reality by changing your inner beliefs and attitudes.

Gift 37: Your dominant thoughts will attract into your life the people and circumstances you need, when and in the form you need.

Gift 38: Many would rather be ruined by praise than saved by criticism.

Gift 39: We have Ph.D.s in other people's business but need tutoring in our own.

Gift 40: You can be a role model by teaching someone through your magnificence or through your miscues.

Gift 41: Treat every day like you have not done your best work yet.

Plus Gift: We should eat the dessert first sometimes.

Plus Gift: Don't sensor your words, your spirit or your thoughts.

Plus Gift: Take fuel along on your journey.

Plus Gift: Don't get even, get ahead... let personal and professional happiness be your panacea.

PERSONAL AWESOME ACTION PAGE

Write your key action steps below. When you're finished, quickly return to the next chapter and read more about what it takes to move from AVERAGE to AWESOME:

1 File, Save, Open, and Print

    1. _____

    2. _____

    3. _____

    4. _____

    5. _____

2 Savor Your Moments

    1. _____

    2. _____

    3. _____

    4. _____

    5. _____

3 Remember Your Titans

    1. _____

    2. _____

    3. _____

    4. _____

    5. _____

4   Get Mad, Get Sad, Get Better, Get Busy

1. _____
2. _____
3. _____
4. _____
5. _____

5   Ready, Aim, Fire Up an Awesome Day!

1. _____
2. _____
3. _____
4. _____
5. _____

6   Fire Hard, Kid!

1. _____
2. _____
3. _____
4. _____
5. _____

7   Start Playing More Reader Rabbit!

1. _____
2. _____
3. _____
4. _____
5. _____

8   Stop Depositing Bad Checks

1. _____
2. _____
3. _____
4. _____
5. _____

9   Say Cheese!

1. _____
2. _____
3. _____
4. _____
5. _____

10   Wear Your Own Jersey

1. _____
2. _____
3. _____
4. _____
5. _____

11   Say What You Mean and Mean What You Say

1. _____
2. _____
3. _____
4. _____
5. _____

12   Let Your Light Shine

1. _____
2. _____
3. _____
4. _____
5. _____

13   Believe You Can Fly

1. _____
2. _____
3. _____
4. _____
5. _____

14   Some People are Just Not Going to Clap

1. _____
2. _____
3. _____
4. _____
5. _____

15   Be Yourself, Because Everyone Else Is Taken

1. _____
2. _____
3. _____
4. _____
5. _____

16   You're Not Always Going to Get the Best Hand

1. _____
2. _____
3. _____
4. _____
5. _____

17   Sssssshhhh…Listen to Your Own Advice

1. _____
2. _____
3. _____
4. _____
5. _____

18   Have a Forgiving Spirit

1. _____
2. _____
3. _____
4. _____
5. _____

19   Remember That the Cure for the Pain is in the Pain

1. _____
2. _____
3. _____
4. _____
5. _____

20   **Start With the Wing First!**

1. _____
2. _____
3. _____
4. _____
5. _____

21   **Know that It's Not Always All About You**

1. _____
2. _____
3. _____
4. _____
5. _____

22   **Dance Like Nobody's Watching**

1. _____
2. _____
3. _____
4. _____
5. _____

23   **Listen to the Music**

1. _____
2. _____
3. _____
4. _____
5. _____

24   Be Hungreee!

1. _____
2. _____
3. _____
4. _____
5. _____

25   Keep Your Glasses Clean

1. _____
2. _____
3. _____
4. _____
5. _____

26   Wow Yourself!

1. _____
2. _____
3. _____
4. _____
5. _____

27   Get the Junk Out of YOUR Trunk

1. _____
2. _____
3. _____
4. _____
5. _____

28   Enjoy Your Awesome Journey!

1. _____
2. _____
3. _____
4. _____
5. _____

29   Understand That Awesome Challenges ALWAYS Await You

1. _____
2. _____
3. _____
4. _____
5. _____

TAKE THE 30-DAY AWESOME CHALLENGE

Take your Awesome Action Steps and write below the top ten steps you're going to work on immediately, within the next 30 days. Develop a 30-Day Awesome Action Plan! Determine what resources you're going to need. Determine how you're going to measure your results. In addition, determine how you're going to WOW yourself upon completion. If you like, you can email your plan to me at: jimsmith@jimpactenterprises.com and let me know how things are going! I'd love to read about your success.

Next, develop Awesome Action Plans for the next ten, then the next ten, etc. I wish you the very best as you continue your awesome journey! Don't forget to have some fun along the way!

My Top Ten Awesome Next Steps:

1. _____
2. _____
3. _____
4. _____
5. _____
6. _____
7. _____
8. _____
9. _____
10. _____

My Awesome Action Plan:

_____

_____

_____

_____

_____

What Resources I am going to need:

_____

_____

_____

_____

_____

How I'm going to measure my results:

_____

_____

_____

_____

_____

How I'm going to WOW myself upon completion:

_____

_____

_____

_____

_____

My Top Ten Awesome Next Steps:

1. _____
2. _____
3. _____
4. _____
5. _____
6. _____
7. _____
8. _____
9. _____
10. _____

My Awesome Action Plan:

_____
_____
_____
_____
_____

What Resources I am going to need:

_____
_____
_____
_____
_____

How I'm going to measure my results:

_____

_____

_____

_____

_____

How I'm going to WOW myself upon completion:

_____

_____

_____

_____

_____

ABOUT THE AUTHOR

Jim Smith, Jr., according to the many thousands who have participated in his moving motivational keynote presentations and workshops, is one of the most energetic and passionate speakers who have come along in recent time. He really connects with his audiences, encouraging them and challenging them to be outstanding. His speaking style evolved, he says, from his ups and downs in corporate America, education, professional and college sports, parenting and marriage. It's this awesome journey that has taken him from a small, second floor, two-bedroom apartment in West Philadelphia to inspiring and motivating both national and international audiences.

Upon graduation from college with a degree in English, Jim, after months of receiving form letters of decline, secured his first corporate opportunity. Prior to putting on the suit and tie every day, however, Jim set his sights on professional football, a dream he held for some time. He realized his other sports dream, winning a National College

Football Championship, during his junior year. He vividly remembers sitting in the stands all teary-eyed when the Philadelphia Stars cut him, and his dream, from the team. He knew, however, that many more of his dreams would come to fruition. And he was right!

From Average to Awesome: 41 Plus *Gifts in 41* Plus *Years* is his first book.

To find out more about Jim and the services he provides through JIMPACT Enterprises please visit the Company website at:
www.jimpact.com